FEBRUARY

M	T	W	T	F	S	S
	1	2	3	4	5	6
7	8	9	10	11	12	13
14	15	16	17	18	19	20
21	22	23	24	25	26	27
28						

APRIL

M	T	W	T	F	S	S
				1	2	3
4	5	6	7	8	9	10
11	12	13	14	15	16	17
18	19	20	21	22	23	24
25	26	27	28	29	30	

JUNE

M	T	W	T	F	S	S
		1	2	3	4	5
6	7	8	9	10	11	12
13	14	15	16	17	18	19
20	21	22	23	24	25	26
27	28	29	30			

THE
ALMANAC

THE
ALMANAC

A SEASONAL GUIDE TO
2022

LIA LEENDERTZ

With illustrations by Harry Brockway

First published in Great Britain in 2021 by Gaia,
an imprint of Octopus Publishing Group Ltd
Carmelite House
50 Victoria Embankment
London EC4Y 0DZ
www.octopusbooks.co.uk

An Hachette UK Company
www.hachette.co.uk

Text copyright © Lia Leendertz 2021
Design and layout copyright © Octopus Publishing Group Ltd 2021
Illustrations copyright © Harry Brockway 2021
Music copyright © Richard Barnard 2021

ISBN 978-1-85675-470-5

A CIP catalogue record for this book is available from the British Library.

Printed and bound in the United Kingdom.

10 9 8 7 6 5 4 3 2 1

Publisher: Stephanie Jackson
Creative Director: Jonathan Christie
Designer: Matt Cox at Newman+Eastwood
Editor: Ella Parsons
Copy Editor: Alison Wormleighton
Senior Production Manager: Peter Hunt

Ovens should be preheated to the specific temperature – if using a
fan-assisted oven, follow manufacturer's instructions for adjusting the
time and the temperature. Pepper should be freshly ground black
pepper unless otherwise stated.

This FSC® label means that materials used for the
product have been responsibly sourced.

CONTENTS

INTRODUCTION

Hello and welcome to *The Almanac: A Seasonal Guide to 2022*. If you are new to *The Almanac*, then I hope you will enjoy following the coming year through these pages, and if you are a regular reader, then I am delighted to welcome you back.

As ever, you will find a mixture of core seasonal information – sunrises and sunsets, moon phases, tide times – albeit in new formats, and some other ways of looking at the unfolding year. I like to have a theme to each issue and this year it is folk celebrations, the ways that people gather to mark out the year, every one of them alive and kicking – fingers crossed – in 2022. I make no judgements about these celebrations: many may not be rooted in true historic gatherings and will have had their meanings changed over the years. The lineage of such things is kinked and imperfect, yet people will gather together to celebrate the seasons, and that seems like a wonderful thing to me. Goodness knows, we need to take every opportunity to get together and dress up, dance, laugh, eat and sing. I have had great fun tracking down the folk songs, stories and recipes that are tied to these gatherings, and I hope they provide you with some new ways of marking the year, even if you are not able to attend in person.

Many of you have told me that you have found solace in *The Almanac* over the past couple of turbulent years, and comfort in the natural world when everything has been in flux. This almanac will tell you the best moments to pick out distant star clusters, or to push tiny seeds into the earth. Somehow both activities have a similar effect on me, grounding me and reminding me of greater forces, of patterns that go on. Remember that whatever happens, the sun will rise in the east and set in the west, the moon will move through its phases, the tides will pull themselves up the shore and fall away again, and the biscuit of the month will need to be baked. Have a wonderful 2022.

Lia Leendertz

NOTES ON USING *THE ALMANAC*

Geographical and cultural scope

The geographical scope of this almanac covers Britain and Ireland. The cultural scope is the stories, songs, food, travels and festivities of all the people who live within them.

The sky at night

The events within the sky at night section generally fall into three categories: eclipses, meteor showers and close approaches of the moon to a naked-eye planet or of two naked-eye planets to each other.

While the first two categories are self-explanatory, the third will benefit from a little clarification. The naked-eye planets are those planets that can be easily seen with the naked eye. They are generally very bright, as bright as the brightest stars, and this makes them relatively easy to spot, even in cities where sky-spotting conditions are not ideal. From brightest to dimmest they are: Venus, Jupiter, Mars and Saturn. Those not included in this almanac are Mercury, Neptune and Uranus. Mercury is very hard to spot because it is close to the sun and therefore is usually lost in its glare. Neptune and Uranus can only be spotted with a strong telescope.

A 'close approach' means that two of them, or one of them plus the moon, are in the same part of the sky. They are, of course, nowhere near each other in reality, but to us, they look as if they are. This can make them easier to spot than they would be when they are lone-ranging across the sky.

Planets are generally visible for weeks or even months in similar parts of the sky each night, but to help you find them easily, any dates given in these sections are for when they are in close proximity to the moon or each other, or when they are particularly bright.

To identify the part of the sky where they will most easily be seen, I have given the best time to spot them, plus a compass point and the altitude. The time is important because the sky wheels around us as the night wears on. The altitude is given in degrees: the horizon is 0 degrees and straight up is 90 degrees.

Sunrise and sunset

This year the sunrise and sunset charts include the times for the start of morning twilight (when the sun is 18 degrees below the horizon), sunrise (which is when morning twilight ends), sunset (which is when evening twilight starts) and the end of evening twilight (when the sun is 18 degrees below the horizon).

Tides

The tide timetables this year are in a new, visual format that should make it easy to convert them for your local port. A full tide timetable is given each month for Dover, because Dover is widely used as a standard port from which to work out all other tide times. Every port has a 'high water time difference on Dover' figure, which you can find on the internet. For instance, Bristol's high water time difference on Dover is –4h 10m, and so, looking at this almanac's visual tide timetable, you would just trace your finger back along it 4 hours and 10 minutes to see that a midday high tide at Dover would mean it will be high tide at Bristol at 7.50am. London Bridge's high water time difference on Dover is +2h 52m, so, tracing forwards, a midday high tide at Dover would see a high tide in London at 2.52pm. Once you know any local port's figure, you can just trace that amount of time backwards or forwards along the Dover tide line.

Here are a few ports and their high water time differences on Dover. Find your local one by searching the name of the port and the phrase 'high water time difference on Dover'.

Aberdeen:	+2h 31m	Cork:	–5h 23m
Firth of Forth:	+3h 50m	Swansea:	–4h 50m
Port Glasgow:	+1h 32m	Bristol:	–4h 10m
Newcastle-upon-Tyne:	+4h 33m	London Bridge:	+2h 52m
Belfast Lough:	+0h 7m	Lyme Regis:	–4h 55m
Hull:	–4h 52m	Newquay:	–6h 4m
Liverpool:	+0h 14m	St Helier, Jersey:	–4h 55m

Do not use these where accuracy is critical; instead, you will need to buy a local tide timetable, or subscribe to Easy Tide, www.ukho.gov.uk/easytide. Also note that no timetable will take into account the effects of wind and barometric pressure.

Spring tide and neap tide dates are also included. Spring tides are the most extreme tides of the month – the highest and lowest tides – and neap tides are the least extreme. Spring tides happen as a result of the pull that occurs when the sun, moon and earth are aligned. Alignment occurs at new moon and full moon, but the surge – the spring tide – is slightly delayed because of the mass of water to be moved. It usually follows one to three days after. Knowledge of spring tides is particularly useful if you are a keen rock-pooler, beachcomber or mudlark. You want a low spring tide for best revelations.

Gardening by the moon

In past years I have included some basic information on gardening by the moon, and this year I have delved deeper into the various moon gardening methods in order to give a lot more detail, outlining which jobs to attempt at different phases of the moon throughout the year.

Some people believe that, just as the moon moves the earth's water to create the tides, it has other effects on the natural world. If it can move oceans, perhaps it can move ground water, too, and even the water trapped in each plant. Planting by the moon is a method of gardening that taps into the rising and falling of water with the moon's phases, in practical terms but also in the more mystical sense of drawing up and drawing down energy as the moon waxes and wanes.

This almanac makes no claims on the efficacy of gardening by the moon, but if you wish to give it a try, the relevant dates and jobs are included for each month. And even if you are not interested in this approach, the sections will also work well as straightforward guides to monthly jobs in the garden.

January

1 New Year's Day

3 Bank holiday in lieu of New Year's Day – England, Scotland, Wales, Northern Ireland, Ireland

4 Bank holiday, Scotland

5 Twelfth Night (Christian)

6 Epiphany/Three Kings' Day/Little Christmas (Christian)

6 Nollaig na mBan/Women's Christmas (Christian/Irish tradition)

6 Orthodox Christmas Eve (Orthodox)

7 Orthodox Christmas Day (Orthodox)

7 Lidat (Rastafarian)

10 Plough Monday (English traditional)

13 Lohri (Punjabi winter festival)

17 Old Twelfth Night (traditional)

25 Burns Night (Scottish traditional)

29 29th–30th: Big Garden Birdwatch

31 Chinese New Year's Eve

DRESSING UP IN JANUARY

The Holly Man of Bankside

In the bare and brown winter, holly glows glossy and green and is covered in deep red berries. It perhaps is no surprise that this plant has come to personify winter in myth and folklore.

The Holly Man is at the centre of London Bankside's Twelfth Night celebrations. Also known as the Holly King, he is the traditional personification of winter: an old man with white hair and beard, wearing a green cloak and a holly crown. The timing of his rise and fall is flexible, depending on tradition and story. In some Wiccan and neopagan traditions he is born in the autumn, is at the height of his powers at midwinter and then is killed off in the spring when his summer counterpart, the Oak King (or Green Man, or any number of other names – see page 96), is ascendant. Spring will bring a great battle between these two foes, but right now, the Holly King rules.

Throughout the British Isles people love to dress up and celebrate their folklore and the seasons. While many of these celebrations have genuinely been handed down through the ages, others are Victorian inventions, and some are modern takes. A great many are a mixture of all three. They may not meet the standards of historical purists, but each is rowdy and lively and repeated year after year, and each marks the month in its own way. Twelve of the figures at the centre of these celebrations are celebrated in this almanac, by way of an introduction to the month in which they fall.

The arrival of the Holly Man over the Thames to Bankside via the Millennium Bridge, accompanied by wassailing, is part of the Twelfth Night celebrations run by a group of actors called The Lions Part. The festivities include elements associated with medieval Twelfth Night merrymaking, which acted as a last blast of celebration before Plough Monday, the day to return to work. A mummers' play is performed outside Shakespeare's Globe Theatre. Cakes are distributed among the crowd, one cake containing a dried pea and one a dried bean, with the lucky recipients crowned King and Queen – after which the revellers enjoy mulled wine, dancing and storytelling at the 17th-century George Inn in Borough High Street.

THE SKY

There is some action in the sky at night early in the month, with the Quadrantids meteor shower – one of the most reliable of the year – putting on its show on a good dark-moon night. Venus, which can only ever be seen in the morning or evening, will be a morning star for the first months of the year, so look out at dawn. Jupiter will bow out as an evening star early next month, so take the chance to see it now.

At night

3rd–4th: Quadrantids meteor shower. Best time for viewing will be from late evening on the 3rd, when the radiant will be at an altitude of 20 degrees in the northeast, and on into the early hours of the 4th. As we will be just past the new moon, there will be no interference from moonlight, so it could be a good display.

6th: Close approach of Jupiter and the crescent moon. They will first appear in the dusk at about 16.30 above the southern horizon at an altitude of 24 degrees. They set in the southwest at 20.00.

By day

4th: Perihelion. This is the moment in the year when the earth is nearest the sun in its elliptical orbit. At 06.52 the sun will be 147,105,052km away (compare with aphelion on 4th July, see page 143).

21st: At solar noon the sun will reach an altitude of 18 degrees in the London sky and 14 degrees in the Glasgow sky.

1st–31st: Day length increases this month by 1h 19m at Clitheroe, Lancashire.

Sunrise and set
Clitheroe, Lancashire

	01	02	03	04	05	06	07	08	09	10	11	12	13	14	15	16	17	18	19	20	21	22	23	24
1st																								
2nd																								
3rd																								
4th																								
5th																								
6th																								
7th																								
8th																								
9th																								
10th																								
11th																								
12th																								
13th																								
14th																								
15th																								
16th																								
17th																								
18th																								
19th																								
20th																								
21st																								
22nd																								
23rd																								
24th																								
25th																								
26th																								
27th																								
28th																								
29th																								
30th																								
31st																								

Deep-sky objects

The Orion Nebula/Messier 42

In a reasonably dark sky there are around two dozen 'deep-sky objects' (astronomical bodies outside our solar system and consisting of more than a single star) that can be seen without binoculars or a telescope. We are talking here about being able to pick out nebulae, galaxies and star clusters with the naked eye.

The Orion Nebula, also called Messier 42 or M42 (after French astronomer Charles Messier, who catalogued 110 deep-sky objects), is one of the easier ones to find, tucked as it is within well-known Orion, which is high in the sky throughout winter. Look for a line of stars hanging down from Orion's belt like a sword. The nebula is a fuzzy patch of blue at the centre of these. You are looking at a stellar nursery about 1,350 light years away from us and around 24 light years across. It contains at least 700 stars in various stages of formation.

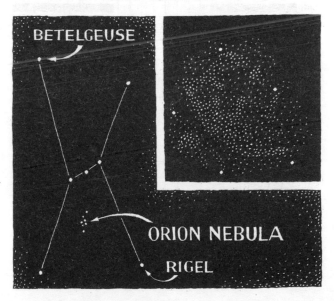

BETELGEUSE

ORION NEBULA

RIGEL

THE SEA

Average sea temperature

Shetland:	8.9°C
Greenock:	8.2°C
Cleethorpes:	6.6°C
Rhyl:	7.7°C
Rosslare:	9.6°C
Bideford:	9.0°C
Deal:	7.6°C

Spring and neap tides

Spring tides are the most extreme tides of the month, with the highest rises and the lowest falls, and they follow a couple of days after the full moon and new moon. There will be a super new moon (when the new moon coincides with the moment in the month when the moon is closest to the earth) on the 2nd so the spring tides that follow may be more extreme than usual. Neap tides are the least extreme tides of the month, with the smallest movement, and they fall in between the spring tides.

Spring tides: 4th–6th and 19th–21st

Neap tides: 13th–14th and 28th–29th

Spring tides are shaded in black in the chart opposite.

January tide timetable for Dover

For guidance on how to convert this for your local area, see page 8.

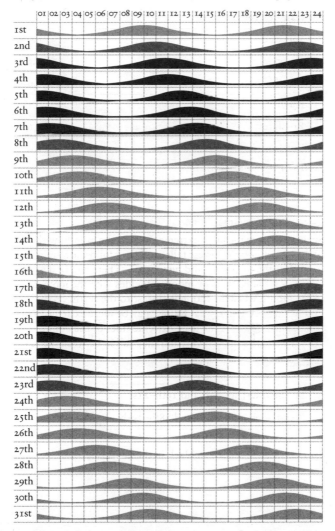

THE MOON

Moon phases

New moon – 2nd January, 18.33

1st quarter – 9th January, 18.11

Full moon – 17th January, 23.48

3rd quarter – 25th January, 13.40

Full moon
Names for January's full moon: Wolf Moon, Stay at Home Moon.

New moon
This month's new moon is in Capricorn. Astrologers believe that the new moon is a good time to make plans and focus on your dreams and hopes for the period ahead, and that each new moon has a particular energy, depending on which zodiacal sign it is in. The Capricorn new moon, which falls on the 2nd, is said to rule ambitions and goals, making this a good time to think about career plans and changes and how you can start to work towards them.

Moon phases for January

1st	2nd NEW	3rd	4th	5th

6th	7th	8th	9th	10th

11th	12th	13th	14th	15th

16th	17th FULL	18th	19th	20th

21st	22nd	23rd	24th	25th

26th	27th	28th	29th	30th

31st

THE GARDEN

Gardening by the moon

Just as the moon moves the earth's water to create tides, some people believe that it has other effects on the natural world as well. If the moon can move oceans, perhaps it can move ground water, too, and maybe even the tiny amounts of water inside plant cells. There are several different methods of moon gardening, but in this one different jobs are apportioned to the four phases of the moon, taking into account the combined or opposing pull that the sun and moon have on the earth, and the increasing and decreasing light as the moon waxes and wanes.

In January, light and temperatures are still low – in fact, this is often the coldest month of the year – and much of the necessary work falls neatly into the 'dormant' phase of the month. There is lots of maintenance, planning and preparation to be done for the season ahead, but there are also the very first sowings to get underway and the potatoes to chit.

Whether you are gardening in time with the moon or not, use the following as a guide to jobs to do in January.

Note: Sometimes these dates differ from those in the moon phase chart on page 19, to take into account sensible gardening hours. Where no specific time for the change between phases is mentioned, this is because it happens early in the morning or late at night. For exact changeover times for any late-night or pre-dawn gardening, refer to the moon phase chart.

3rd quarter to new moon: 1st–2nd and 25th (from 13.40)–31st
A dormant period, with low sap and poor growth. Do not sow or plant. Prune, weed and harvest crops for storage. Fertilise and mulch. Garden maintenance.
- Prune apple, pear, medlar and quince trees. Prune autumn-fruiting raspberries, red and white currants and gooseberries.
- Winter prune wisteria.

- Clean and oil tools. Clean pots.
- Check your soil for its pH level and add lime or calcified seaweed if necessary.
- Weed and mulch beds ahead of spring.

New moon to 1st quarter: 3rd–9th

Rising vitality and upward growth. Plant and sow anything that develops above ground towards the end of the phase. Prepare for growth.

- Sow chillies and aubergines, broad beans, peas and sweet peas now, or wait for the 1st quarter phase, which is even more suited to sowing.
- Buy seeds, seed trays and compost.
- Place forcers over rhubarb plants.

1st quarter to full moon: 10th–17th

Sow crops that develop above ground, don't sow root crops. Plant out seedlings and young plants. Take cuttings and make grafts. Avoid any other pruning. Fertilise.

- Sow chillies and aubergines in a heated propagator.
- Sow broad beans straight into the ground.
- Sow hardy peas and sweet peas in pots under cover.

Full moon to 3rd quarter: 18th–25th (till 13.40)

A 'drawing down' energy. Sow and plant crops that develop below ground: root crops, bulbs and perennials.

- Plant garlic and rhubarb crowns.
- Sow onions and leeks in seed trays in a heated propagator.
- Plant fruit trees and bushes, hedging and bare-root rosebushes.
- Chit seed potatoes.

THE KITCHEN

Traditionally the season of Christmastide continued on into the beginning of January, ending in the great riotous feast of Twelfth Night, and one last great culinary hurrah seems a much more humane way to crawl through some of the darkest and coldest days of the year than embarking on a New Year diet. There is a great influx of beautiful citrus from the Mediterranean this month, including the Seville oranges we need if we are to fill our cupboards with homemade marmalade. The very first stems of the Yorkshire rhubarb start to arrive, and, of course, there are the less loved Christmas remnants to push through this month, from leftover panettone to the toffee pennies from the bottom of the Quality Street box.

In season

In the hedgerows, woods and fields
Wild greens: Chickweed, hairy bittercress, dandelion leaves, sow thistle, wintercress/yellow rocket
Game: Pheasant, goose, rabbit, venison

From the seashore and rivers
Fish and shellfish: Mussels, oysters, scallops, turbot, cod, whiting, Dover sole, haddock, pollock, bass

From the kitchen garden
Vegetables: Forced rhubarb, purple sprouting broccoli, carrots, Brussels sprouts, turnips, beetroot, spinach, kale, chard, leeks, Jerusalem artichokes, lettuces, chicory, radicchio, endive, cauliflowers, cabbages, celeriac, swedes
Herbs: Winter savory, parsley, chervil, coriander, rosemary, bay, sage

From the farms
Stilton, Lanark Blue

And traditional imports
Seville oranges, Bergamot oranges, Meyer lemons, the first blood oranges, truffles, Gruyère

RECIPES

Biscuit of the month

Cavallucci di Siena – Italian Twelfth Night biscuits
This ancient recipe has long been eaten in Tuscany on Twelfth Night. The spicing is strange but wonderful. Only make this if you have an accurate digital sugar thermometer.

Makes 16
Ingredients
50g walnuts
180g self-raising flour
25g diced candied orange peel
1 ½ teaspoons anise seeds or fennel seeds
1 teaspoon ground cinnamon
Pinch of ground cloves
150g light brown sugar
50ml water

Method
Preheat the oven to 160°C, Gas Mark 3. Put the walnuts on a baking sheet and toast for 20 minutes. Remove, cool and chop, then combine in a bowl with the flour, candied peel, anise or fennel seeds, cinnamon and cloves. Dissolve the sugar in the water in a saucepan, and heat until it has reached 106°–112°C, or the 'thread stage' (when drizzled into a glass of water, it forms threads or clumps at the bottom of the glass). Tip the flour mixture into the saucepan and mix with the syrup to form a sticky dough.

Once the dough is cool enough to handle, turn it onto a lightly floured surface, and form into a sausage shape. Divide into 4 pieces then form each piece into 4 ovals, placing them on a baking sheet lined with nonstick baking paper, and flattening them slightly. They do not grow a huge amount so you can probably fit all 16 onto one tray. Bake for 15 minutes, then leave to cool completely.

Pink grapefruit and rosemary Caipirinha

The vibrant Brazilian cocktail Caipirinha can be adapted to make use of some of the winter citrus that is now around. It is traditionally made with just lime, but you can add any citrus you like; it will all work beautifully as long as you choose fruits on the sharp, sour side. *Cachaça* is distilled from fresh sugar cane juice and is Brazil's national spirit, but if you can't track it down you can use white rum (in which case the cocktail is called a Caipirissima, strictly speaking). The addition of rosemary is entirely inauthentic, but it makes the drink more wintry, and perhaps more suited to a northern January. In the summer you could do the same with a handful of mint leaves.

Serves 4

Ingredients

2 limes

¼ pink grapefruit, cut into 8 pieces

Sprig of rosemary

6 tablespoons golden caster sugar

About 850g crushed ice

200ml *cachaça* or white rum

Method

Roll the limes on your worktop under the flat of your hand, pushing down hard to break the membranes that hold the juice. Cut into quarters. Tip the limes and grapefruit into a large jug, then bend and crush the rosemary and add it, too, followed by the sugar. Spend a couple of minutes using the end of a rolling pin to muddle and crush together the sugar, fruit and herbs. Tip in enough of the crushed ice to fill the jug to about a third, and then crush and muddle again. Add the *cachaça* or white rum and the rest of the ice, stir and serve in Old Fashioned glasses.

FOLK STORY OF THE MONTH

The Farmer and the Boggart

The first Monday after Epiphany is Plough Monday, which in 2022 falls on 10th January. This was the traditional start of the English agricultural year and the day when work resumed after Christmas. Here is a very old tale said to originate in Lincolnshire, about a farmer ploughing and tilling his land, and outwitting a boggart – a malevolent spirit – in the process.

There was once a strong, handsome, hardworking farmer. The harvests were good for several years, and he saved up a little money so that when the fallow field alongside his farm came up for sale, he bought it. That night, he called to his wife, 'I am so happy to own the new field. We shall get a good crop this year.'

They were both shocked to hear a low, growly voice say, 'But it ain't yours, is it?' There, next to the fire, was a boggart – squat, hairy and strongly built. He told them that the field belonged to him, and that it had produced no crops for many years because the farmer wouldn't give him his fair share. Now, our farmer was canny and knew that a deal had to be made, so he asked the boggart what he required. 'I own the field, and you do the work,' said the boggart, 'so we should split the crop half and half.' 'Deal,' said the farmer. 'What do you want to take the first year then? The tops or the bottoms?' The boggart laughed as if it was obvious. 'Why, I'll take the tops, of course!'

The next day the farmer went out and sowed his field with turnips. At harvest time the boggart came to collect his half and the farmer presented him with a cartful of turnip tops. The boggart was furious, but the farmer reminded him of their deal and said, 'What will you have next year?' 'Why the bottoms, of course!' shouted the boggart. The farmer sowed his field with barley. Come harvest time, when the boggart came to collect his share the farmer presented him with a field full of stubble. The boggart stamped and raged and then stomped off away from the field, knowing he was beaten. He was never seen again.

FOLK SONG OF THE MONTH

'Here We Come A-Wassailing'
Traditional, arr. Richard Barnard

This is a traditional wassailing song for Twelfth Night.
There were two distinct types of wassailing. One involved
moving from door to door singing and carrying a wassail
bowl, and the other was held in orchards, singing to and
blessing the trees for a fruitful year ahead. It is the second
type that is now more widespread, the rise in community
orchards sparking a revival, so look out for one near you
on or around Twelfth Night.

Here we come a-wassailing among the leaves so green,
Here we come a-wassailing so fair to be seen.
Love and joy come to you
And to you a wassail too,
And God bless you and send you a happy New Year
And God send you a happy New Year!

Call up the master of the house, put on his golden ring,
Bring us all a glass of ale and better we shall sing.
Love and joy come to you etc.

We have a little purse and it is made of leather skin,
We want a silver sixpence to line it well within.
Love and joy come to you etc.

God bless the master of the house and bless the mistress
too,
And all the little children that round the table go.
Love and joy come to you etc.

NATURE

Bird of the month – robin

If you hear silvery, lyrical birdsong on a January evening, there is a good chance it will be a robin, seeking its mate. Both male and female robins sing, and they do so all year round, making them one of the few birds to keep on singing through the depths of winter. Their large eyes mean they are well attuned to dusky light, and they are often among the first birds to start singing in the morning and the last to stop at night. They sing tuneful, slightly melancholy phrases followed by longer pauses, with the tone decidedly sadder and more wistful in autumn, and more energetic, upbeat and powerful in spring. The 'spring' song starts as early as mid-December and so is in full flow by now. Robins stop singing only briefly in the summer when they are moulting and not looking their best.

The primary purpose of all of this singing is to defend their territories, and they are among the few birds to hold a territory year round. A breeding territory will be defended by a pair through summer, and is about 0.55 hectares in size, while a winter territory is defended by an individual and is about half that size. A male will respond to any patch of red when defending his territory, with fights between two males vicious and often to the death.

The song is also used to attract mates, of course, and robins will pair up in the depths of winter. Soon after, the female will build a cup-shaped nest in a fully concealed nook close to the ground.

The red breast supposedly came about when a brown robin was splashed with Christ's blood as it sang to comfort him when he was dying on the cross. Robins have long been considered to have a connection to the spirit world, and to be able to pass on messages from loved ones who have died. Perhaps this is down to their relaxed and companionable behaviour around people, often keeping us company in the garden as we upturn the earth to provide them with worms.

ROBIN · MATURE · RED BREAST · JUVENILE · SPECKLED PLUMAGE · PALE BLUE EGGS

February

1	Chinese New Year/Spring Festival/Lunar New Year – Year of the Tiger begins
1	St Brigid's Day (Christian)
1	Start of LGBT+ History Month
1	1st–2nd: Imbolc (Gaelic/pagan/neopagan)
2	Candlemas (Christian)
4	Start of Winter Olympic Games, Beijing
5	Vasant Panchami (Hindu spring festival)
14	St Valentine's Day
15	Parinirvana Day/Nirvana Day (Buddhist)

DRESSING UP IN FEBRUARY

Lion dancing and red underwear for Chinese New Year

Chinese New Year is the most important celebration of the year in China and many other Asian countries, and is also widely celebrated around the world wherever people from China have settled, including the UK and Ireland. There are major Chinese New Year celebrations in London's Chinatown as well as in Chinatowns in Manchester, Birmingham, Newcastle and Liverpool, with many smaller celebrations elsewhere.

In China it is commonly called Spring Festival. This feels a little optimistic for chilly February, but the days are lengthening and spring is on its way. You can see it in the flowering of the snowdrops and hear it in the increase in birdsong. This year it falls on Tuesday, 1st February, and it marks the beginning of the Year of the Tiger.

The Lion dancers are one of the main attractions at any Chinese New Year celebration. Two dancers make up a lion, with one taking the highly decorated head and the other playing the back half, like a pantomime horse. The vigorous and energetic movements come from martial arts, and the music is a loud drum beat, with cymbals and gongs. Troupes will visit local homes and shops and take part in the traditional custom of Cai Qing ('plucking the greens'). An envelope stuffed with greenery such as lettuce is left out for the lion, as well as a red envelope full of money for the troupe. The lion eats and spits out the green envelope and keeps the red one.

Every element of Chinese New Year, from the clothes worn to the food eaten, is heavy with symbolism in order to bring good luck for the New Year. The Lion dancers are symbolic of power, prosperity, wisdom and luck, and the dances are performed to bring good fortune and chase away evil spirits for the year ahead. For everyone else, it is traditional to wear brand-new red clothing – and particularly red underwear – on the first day of New Year. Red is an auspicious colour and brings luck, happiness and energy.

THE SKY

This month will see the final brief evening showing of Jupiter in 2022 before it is lost in the glare of the sun. It will reappear as a morning star in the summer. Venus can still be seen in the sky at dawn.

At night

2nd: Close approach of Jupiter and the moon. First appearing in the dusk at about 17.20 above the southwestern horizon at an altitude of 9 degrees. They set in the west–southwest at 18.20.

By day

21st: At solar noon the sun will reach an altitude of 28 degrees in the London sky and 24 degrees in the Glasgow sky.

1st–28th: Day length increases this month by 1h 54m at Clitheroe, Lancashire.

Sunrise and set
Clitheroe, Lancashire

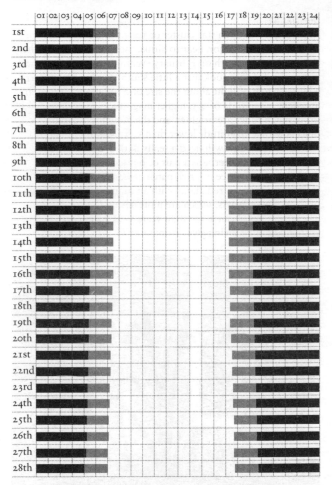

Deep-sky objects

Messier 41

Messier 41 – an open star cluster of 100 or more stars – is located in Canis Major, near to Sirius, the brightest star in the sky. Look to the south on February evenings and, once you find Sirius, the dog star, look just a little south of it for Messier 41, a blurry patch of light about the size of a full moon. It is at an apparent magnitude of 4.5; higher magnitudes are fainter, and lower magnitudes are brighter, and the human eye can only see objects with a magnitude lower than 5, so Messier 41 is fairly faint in the sky. You will need a really dark country sky and clear weather, and perhaps a pair of binoculars.

What you will see is a rich patch of both faint and bright stars, some of them red giants with an orange glow, and some of them white dwarfs, which are more silvery blue in colour. The cluster lies about 2,300 light years away from earth and is estimated to be moving away from us at 23.3km per second.

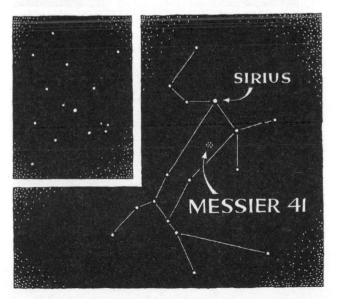

THE SEA

Average sea temperature

Shetland:	8.4°C
Greenock:	7.5°C
Cleethorpes:	6.3°C
Rhyl:	7.4°C
Rosslare:	8.9°C
Bideford:	8.6°C
Deal:	7.6°C

Spring and neap tides

Spring tides are the most extreme tides of the month, with the highest rises and the lowest falls, and they follow a couple of days after the full moon and new moon. Neap tides are the least extreme, with the smallest movement, and they fall in between the spring tides.

Spring tides: 3rd–5th and 18th–20th

Neap tides: 10th–11th and 25th–26th

Spring tides are shaded in black in the chart opposite.

February tide timetable for Dover

For guidance on how to convert this for your local area, see page 8.

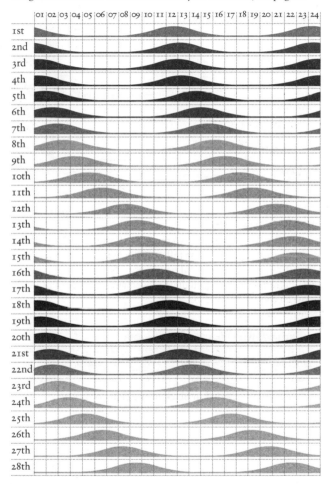

THE MOON

Moon phases

New moon – 1st February, 05.46

1st quarter – 8th February, 13.50

Full moon – 16th February, 16.56

3rd quarter – 23rd February, 22.32

Full moon
Names for February's full moon: Snow Moon, Ice Moon, Storm Moon.

New moon
Each year, the new moon that falls between 21st January and 20th February brings Chinese New Year. This year it falls on 1st February, marking the beginning of the Year of the Tiger.

This month's new moon is in Aquarius. Astrologers believe that the new moon is a good time to make plans and focus on your dreams and hopes for the period ahead, and that each new moon has a particular energy, depending on which zodiacal sign it is in. The Aquarius new moon is said to be an unconventional and trailblazing sign, making this a good time to give your most inventive thoughts and ideas space to breathe.

Moon phases for February

1st NEW	2nd	3rd	4th	5th
6th	7th	8th	9th	10th
11th	12th	13th	14th	15th
16th FULL	17th	18th	19th	20th
21st	22nd	23rd	24th	25th
26th	27th	28th		

THE GARDEN

Gardening by the moon

Although light is increasing, it is still too early for almost all direct sowing: 'As the days grow longer, the cold grows stronger'. Use this time for maintenance and preparation so that, when spring arrives, you are ready to hit the ground running. There are a few things that do benefit from sowing now if you didn't manage them last month, but they will need to be sown in pots in a greenhouse or a cold frame, and some of them in a heated propagator indoors. A fair February is generally thought to mean that winter is going to come back with a vengeance, so if it is still cold, be glad that better is coming soon, and if it is warm and sunny, well, enjoy it while it lasts.

Whether you are gardening in time with the moon or not, use the following as a guide to jobs to do in February.

Note: Sometimes these dates differ from those in the moon phase chart on page 39, to take into account sensible gardening hours. Where no specific time for the change between phases is mentioned, this is because it happens early in the morning or late at night. For exact changeover times for any late-night or pre-dawn gardening, refer to the moon phase chart.

New moon to 1st quarter: 1st–8th (till 13.50)
Rising vitality and upward growth. Plant and sow anything that develops above ground towards the end of the phase. Prepare for growth.
- Sow chillies and aubergines, broad beans and peas if you didn't last month, or wait for the first-quarter phase, which is even more suited to sowing.
- Buy seeds and prepare seed trays or plugs and compost. Get your heated propagator set up.
- Place forcers over rhubarb plants to exclude light and draw up the stems. Give spring cabbages and other brassicas a high-nitrogen feed.

1st quarter to full moon: 8th (from 13.50)–16th

Sow crops that develop above ground, don't sow root crops. Plant out seedlings and young plants. Take cuttings and make grafts. Avoid any other pruning. Fertilise.

- Sow early lettuces, winter salad leaves, spinach, radishes, hardy peas and early varieties of Brussels sprouts, kohlrabi and sprouting broccoli in pots under cover.
- Sow broad beans straight into the ground if it is not frozen and cover them with cloches.
- Sow chillies and aubergines indoors in a heated propagator if you didn't last month.

Full moon to 3rd quarter: 17th–23rd

A 'drawing down' energy. Sow and plant crops that develop below ground: root crops, bulbs and perennials.

- Plant Jerusalem artichokes, garlic, rhubarb crowns and shallot and onions sets.
- Sow onions and leeks in seed trays in a heated propagator.
- Plant fruit trees and bushes, grapevines, hedging and rosebushes.
- Chit seed potatoes.

3rd quarter to new moon: 24th–2nd March

A dormant period, with low sap and poor growth. Do not sow or plant. Prune, weed and harvest crops for storage. Fertilise and mulch the soil. Garden maintenance.

- This is the last chance to prune apple, pear, medlar and quince trees.
- Prune autumn-fruiting raspberries, red and white currants and gooseberries.
- Winter prune wisteria.
- Clean and oil tools. Clean pots.
- Weed beds ahead of spring. Mulch them with organic matter. Prepare for planting out. Pinning clear or black polythene over beds will help warm the soil for early plantings.

NATURE

Bird of the month – thrush

Thrushes are good singers, and blackbirds, which are a species of thrush, start singing their rich and mellow songs early in the year. Here are three you might see in your garden.

The most familiar and common of the thrushes, blackbirds sing between February and June, perched on prominent song posts. They are wonderful singers in a family famed for it, their song arriving in languid and flute-like bursts of six seconds or so with pauses of a similar length in between. It is the youngest males – those hatched the year before – that start singing earliest in the year, with older males joining in later, all staking out their territories. Once the dawn chorus really gets going later in the spring, blackbirds are generally the earliest risers and the first to start the singing each morning. Males are, of course, black, with a yellow bill, and females are brown.

Mistle thrushes start singing even earlier in the year, generally from December onwards. They perch at the top of tall trees and will often sing in very windy conditions, which has earned them the alternative common name 'storm cock'. They are larger than blackbirds, with a greyish brown head and back and a well-speckled underside. In flight they have a pure white underwing.

Song thrushes are similar in colouring and markings to the mistle thrush, but they are smaller birds and coloured a warmer brown, and are more delicately speckled on their undersides. If you find a stone surrounded by lots of smashed snail shells, this indicates the presence of a song thrush, as they are the only birds that use an 'anvil' to remove snails from their shells. Their song is a phrase of a few syllables repeated two to four times.

MISTLE
THRUSH

SONG
THRUSH

BLACKBIRD

THE KITCHEN

Imbolc and St Brigid's Day fall on the 1st February, and both have associations with dairy. So, no matter how grim the month ahead, you have every excuse to start it off with creamy desserts and lashings of butter on everything. In what has traditionally been a mean month for food in Britain, we now have a great feast in the form of Chinese New Year or Spring Festival. Food is a huge part of the celebration and every food has a symbolic meaning: lucky foods that should be eaten on New Year's Eve to guarantee a good year ahead include fish, dumplings, spring rolls, sweet rice balls, glutinous rice cake and tangerines.

In season

In the hedgerows, woods and fields
Wild greens: Chickweed, hairy bittercress, dandelion leaves, sow thistle, wintercress/yellow rocket
Roots: Wild garlic
Game: Rabbit, hare, pheasant, venison

From the seashore and rivers
Fish and shellfish: Mussels, oysters, scallops, turbot, cockles, lemon sole, bass, bream, cod, whiting, haddock

From the kitchen garden
Vegetables: Forced rhubarb, purple sprouting broccoli, carrots, Brussels sprouts, turnips, beetroot, spinach, Jerusalem artichokes, kale, chard, lettuces, chicory, radicchio, puntarelle, endive, cauliflowers, cabbages, celeriac, swedes, leeks
Herbs: Winter savory, parsley, chervil, coriander, rosemary, bay, sage

From the farms
Stilton, Lanark Blue

And traditional imports
Seville oranges, blood oranges, Meyer lemons, Bergamot oranges, Gruyère

RECIPES

Biscuit of the month

Fortune cookies
Make your own personal fortune cookies this Chinese New Year. Prepare the fortunes on slips of paper about 6 x 1cm.

Makes about 16
Ingredients
2 egg whites
½ teaspoon vanilla extract
½ teaspoon almond extract
3 tablespoons sunflower oil
100g plain flour
2 teaspoons cornflour
100g caster sugar

Method
Preheat the oven to 180°C, Gas Mark 4, and line a baking sheet with nonstick baking paper. Put the egg whites, vanilla extract, almond extract and sunflower oil in a bowl and whisk together. In a separate bowl mix the flour, cornflour and sugar, and then sift into the egg mixture. Whisk together and chill for an hour.

Just 2 cookies will be baked at a time so that you have hot, easily shaped cookies to work with. Onto the baking sheet, blob just over ½ tablespoon of mixture. With the back of a spoon, spread it very thin into a round about 8–10cm across. Make a second round. Bake for 8–9 minutes or until the edges turn golden. Place a fortune in the centre and then, because the cookie will be very hot, use 2 knives to fold the cookie in half.

Using a tea towel, lift the cookie and pinch the edges to seal them, then push the straight edge down onto the rim of a mug or glass so that the cookie is folded back the other way. Now push the ends into a hole in a muffin tray to hold them in place while the cookie cools. Repeat with the other cookie, and then repeat the whole process until all of the mixture is used up.

Wild garlic *jiaozi* – pot-sticker dumplings

Dumplings are eaten at the stroke of midnight on Chinese New Year's Eve to bring luck and wealth. Pot stickers are half fried, half steamed, to get both crunch and pillowy softness in each bite.

Wild garlic is starting to appear in February, though it is early for many of us. Use it if you can find it, or substitute with spring onion. You can buy dumpling wrappers in Asian supermarkets or in large supermarkets, if you want to speed things up a bit, but the wrappers are very quick to make.

Makes 16

Ingredients

Wrappers

150g plain flour

Pinch of salt

100ml hot water

Filling

5 tablespoons groundnut or sunflower oil

1 onion, finely diced

50g mushrooms, finely diced

4 garlic cloves, minced

2.5cm piece of fresh root ginger, peeled and grated

100g cabbage, very finely shredded

90g carrots, grated

Large bunch of wild garlic or 50g spring onions, finely shredded (include the greens)

1 tablespoon soy sauce

½ tablespoon rice vinegar

½ tablespoon toasted sesame oil

To fry the dumplings

3 tablespoons groundnut or sunflower oil

Dipping sauce

4 tablespoons soy sauce

1 tablespoon chilli oil

2 tablespoons rice vinegar

1 spring onion, thinly sliced

Method

To make the wrappers, put the flour and salt into a bowl and pour in the hot water little by little, stirring with a fork and adding more water if needed, to make a dough.

Tip the still ragged dough onto a lightly floured surface and knead. Keep kneading for about 5 minutes or until the dough is smooth, then place in a clean bowl, cover and leave to rest for 30 minutes.

Knead again for 5 minutes, then roll into a sausage. Slice this into quarters, and then slice each quarter into quarters, so you have 16 equal pieces. Roll the pieces into balls and then roll the balls out into 9–10cm circles.

To make the filling, put 5 tablespoons of groundnut or sunflower oil into a frying pan over a low-medium heat and cook the onion for about 10 minutes, until starting to soften. Add the mushrooms and cook for a further 10 minutes, stirring occasionally. Add the garlic and ginger and cook for 1 minute or so, then add the cabbage and carrot and cook until tender. Remove from the heat, add the wild garlic or spring onions, soy sauce, rice vinegar and sesame oil, stir and put aside to cool.

Take a wrapper, wet the edges with water, then spoon a generous teaspoon of filling into the centre, forming it into a tidy mound. Fold the wrapper over into a half-moon shape and seal the edges, making a few small pleats along the top by folding little sections a tiny way back on themselves. This will help the dumpling to sit flat on its base – it will look like a tiny Cornish pasty.

Once you have assembled all of the dumplings, put a large nonstick frying pan (one that has a tight-fitting lid, which will be needed later) over a medium heat. Add the 3 tablespoons oil, swirling it around the pan. Add the dumplings, bottoms down, and fry for 3–4 minutes. Tip water into the pan to a depth of 1cm, put the lid on, and steam for 5 minutes. Remove the lid and fry for a couple more minutes or until the bases are crisp and browned.

Mix together the dipping sauce ingredients and serve with the hot dumplings.

FOLK STORY OF THE MONTH

The Nodding Tiger

A poor old lady called Widow T'ang lived with her son in a little one-room shack. They had nothing, but every day the son would go out and cut wood to sell to their neighbours, and in this way they scraped by. One morning he went out, waving a cheery goodbye, but by late evening he hadn't returned. His mother paced and fretted, and in the morning a neighbour set off to look for him. The neighbour hadn't gone far up the mountain when he came across the son's bloodied and torn clothes, and he knew that a tiger had carried him away.

Widow T'ang was beside herself with grief, but rather than sit weeping she walked to the city, stood in front of the magistrate and demanded that the tiger be brought to justice. 'I have lost my son, and have nobody to provide and care for me in my old age. The tiger must be punished!' she said.

The magistrate took pity on her and sent his men out into the forest to hunt for the tiger, but when they found his cave he did not attack them, he simply nodded his head, as if he knew he had done wrong. The men put a strong chain around his neck and led him down the mountain and to the magistrate.

The magistrate – feeling a little silly – asked the tiger if he had eaten Widow T'ang's son. The tiger nodded his head. And so the magistrate said, 'This old woman has nobody to support her. Will you promise to feed her and care for her?' The tiger nodded, so the chain was removed from his neck and he walked peacefully out of the courtroom and back to his cave.

The old woman was furious – she had wanted vengeance, and what good was a tiger's word to her? But the very next day she woke to find a freshly killed deer outside her door, which she butchered and sold at the market. And the tiger kept his promise, delivering food and gifts every week. The old woman grew rich, and in the evenings the tiger would come to the shack and purr as she stroked his fur. They became the best of friends, and the tiger looked after her for the rest of her life.

FOLK SONG OF THE MONTH

'The Lion's Den (The Lady of Carlisle)'
Traditional, arr. Richard Barnard

As we begin the Chinese Year of the Tiger, and to celebrate the Lion dancers that grace every Chinese New Year celebration, here is an English traditional song that mentions both lions and tigers, and an unusual method for finding your true love.

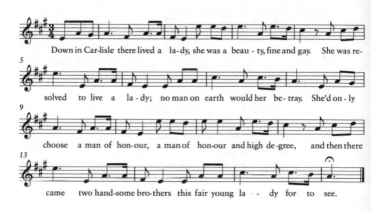

Down in Carlisle there lived a lady,
She was a beauty, fine and gay.
She was resolved to live a lady;
No man on earth would her betray.
She'd only choose a man of honour,
A man of honour and high degree,
And then there came two handsome brothers
This fair young lady for to see.

The first of them a bold sea captain
Belonging to the colonel's corps.
The other was a brave lieutenant
On board the Tiger man-of-war.
She ordered coachmen to get ready
And to the tower they drove, all three,
And there they'd spend one single hour,
The lions and tigers for to see.

The lions and tigers gave such a roaring
And in the den she threw her fan,
Saying 'Which of you, to gain a lady,
Will return my fan again?'
First up spoke the colonel's captain
And said, 'Your offer I can't approve.'
But then spoke loud, the poor lieutenant:
'My life I'll venture for your love.'

And in the den he bravely entered
With lions and tigers fierce and grim
But when they saw his blood was royal
They never touched a hair on him.
And when she saw him come before her,
And no harm to him was done
She laid her head upon his bosom
Saying, 'Here's the prize that you have won.'

March

- **1** Start of meteorological spring
- **1** St David's Day – patron saint of Wales
- **1** Shrove Tuesday – pancake day (Christian/traditional)
- **2** Ash Wednesday – start of Lent (Christian)
- **5** St Piran's Day – patron saint of Cornwall
- **8** International Women's Day
- **8** St John of God's Day – patron saint of booksellers
- **16** 16th–17th: Purim (Jewish)
- **17** St Patrick's Day – patron saint of Ireland – bank holiday, Northern Ireland and Ireland
- **17** 17th–18th: Holi (Hindu spring festival)
- **20** Vernal equinox – start of astronomical spring
- **20** Ostara (neopagan celebration of spring)
- **27** British Summer Time (BST) and Irish Standard Time (IST) begin – both are Universal Coordinated Time (UTC) + 1 hour. Clocks go forward one hour at 01.00
- **27** Mothering Sunday – fourth Sunday in Lent (traditional/Christian)

DRESSING UP IN MARCH

Leprechauns and green for St Patrick's Day

On 17th March throughout Ireland and in areas of the UK with large Irish populations, St Patrick Day parades fill the streets with green hats and clothes and Guinness. The colour of Ireland was not always green – it was once a cool light blue, as depicted in early Irish flags, reflecting the colours worn by St Patrick. But from the Irish Rebellion of 1641 onwards, green flags and clothing started to be carried and worn by Irish revolutionaries, one important element in distinguishing Ireland from the UK and from the colours of the British flag. As Ireland is so verdant that it is known as the Emerald Isle, green certainly feels like its colour.

A good proportion of St Patrick's Day revellers will go a step further and dress as leprechauns. Leprechauns are the 'little people' in Irish mythology, fairy shoemakers. One origin story has them as the diminished remnants of the Tuatha Dé Danann, the pagan, godlike race that ruled pre-Christian Ireland – once they were no longer worshipped, they shrank in size. The word leprechaun is thought possibly to originate from the Old Irish *luchorpán*, in which *lú* means 'small' and *cor* means 'body'.

Cunning and mischievous, they love to trick humans and to hoard gold. The gold dates from the invasion of Ireland by the Danes, who are said to have entrusted their plundered treasure to the leprechauns, who hid it in crocks all around Ireland. You will find a crock at the end of a rainbow, but if you come across a leprechaun and quiz him, he is bound to tell you where it is, just so long as you never take your eyes off him – if you do he will vanish in a moment.

THE SKY

The evening sky is quiet in terms of planets this month.
Venus will rise at its earliest, some two hours before sunrise.
In subsequent months it will get closer to the sun, and it will
become difficult to see from May onwards.

At night

Throughout: Early risers should look out for Venus
in the east, which will rise increasingly close to dawn
from now onwards.

By day

20th: The vernal, or spring, equinox falls at 15.33, the
moment at which the centre of the sun is directly above the
equator, and so day and night are nearly of equal length
all around the globe; this will occur again at the autumn
equinox in September. From today, daylight hours will
continue to lengthen towards the summer solstice.
20th: At solar noon the sun will reach an altitude
of 38 degrees in the London sky and 34 degrees in the
Glasgow sky.
1st–31st: Day length increases this month by 2h 14m at
Clitheroe, Lancashire.

Sunrise and set
Clitheroe, Lancashire

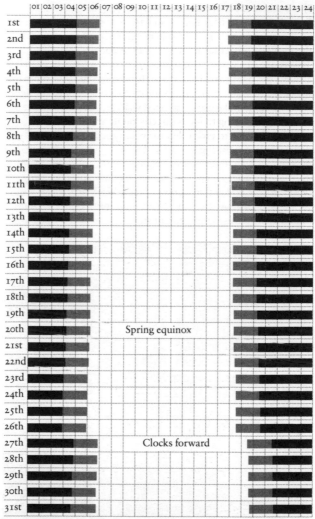

| | 01 | 02 | 03 | 04 | 05 | 06 | 07 | 08 | 09 | 10 | 11 | 12 | 13 | 14 | 15 | 16 | 17 | 18 | 19 | 20 | 21 | 22 | 23 | 24 |

Spring equinox

Clocks forward

British Summer Time and Irish Standard Time begin on 27th March at 01.00 and this has been accounted for above.

Deep-sky objects

The Beehive Cluster/Praesepe/Messier 44

From February to May the constellation of Cancer is high in
the sky in the northern hemisphere. This is the time to look for
the Beehive Cluster (also known as Praesepe or Messier 44).
This is one of the closest star clusters to our solar system, at
around 577 light years from earth. It is large – at three times the
width of the full moon – and appears as a blurry patch of light.

To find it, make use of 'averted vision'. Look around the
area without trying to focus directly on it, and allow your
peripheral vision to pick it out for you. Once you've tracked it
down, look at it through a pair of binoculars or an amateur
telescope. You will see that its brightest stars are bluish-white
in colour. In 2012, scientists discovered two planets orbiting
two sun-like stars in the Beehive Cluster. They are called 'hot
Jupiters': enormous gas giants with high surface temperatures
due to being close to their parent star.

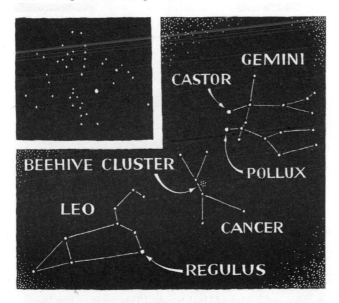

THE SEA

Average sea temperature

Shetland:	8.2°C
Greenock:	7.4°C
Cleethorpes:	6.4°C
Rhyl:	7.4°C
Rosslare:	8.7°C
Bideford:	8.4°C
Deal:	7.2°C

Spring and neap tides

Spring tides are the most extreme tides of the month, with the highest rises and the lowest falls, and they follow a couple of days after the full moon and new moon. Neap tides are the least extreme, with the smallest movement, and they fall in between the spring tides.

Spring tides: 4th–6th and 20th–22nd

Neap tides: 11th–12th and 26th–27th

Spring tides are shaded in black in the chart opposite.

March tide timetable for Dover

For guidance on how to convert this for your local area, see page 8.

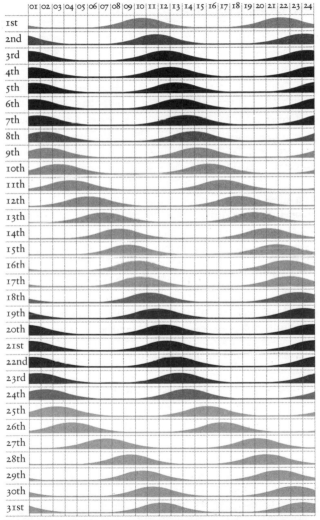

British Summer Time and Irish Standard Time begin on 27th March at 01.00 and this has been accounted for above.

THE MOON

Moon phases

New moon – 2nd March, 17.34

1st quarter – 10th March, 10.45

Full moon – 18th March, 07.17

3rd quarter – 25th March, 05.37

Full moon
Names for March's full moon: Plough Moon, Lenten Moon, Chaste Moon.

New moon
This month's new moon on the 2nd is in Pisces. Astrologers believe that the new moon is a good time to make plans and focus on your dreams and hopes for the period ahead, and that each new moon has a particular energy, depending on which zodiacal sign it is in. Pisces is said to be an intuitive and dreamy sign, making this new moon a time to give space to your imagination, and to make plans to tend to your spiritual health and wellbeing.

Moon phases for March

1st	2nd NEW	3rd	4th	5th
6th	7th	8th	9th	10th
11th	12th	13th	14th	15th
16th	17th	18th FULL	19th	20th
21st	22nd	23rd	24th	25th
26th	27th	28th	29th	30th
31st				

M

THE GARDEN

Gardening by the moon

March brings the equinox and finally we are into the light half of the year, and the garden knows it. Gardening now starts in earnest, but the chance of frost is still extremely high and nights are cold, especially when days are sunny. Caution now will work in your favour.

Whether you are gardening in time with the moon or not, use the following as a guide to jobs to do in March.

Note: Sometimes these dates differ from those in the moon phase chart on page 61, to take into account sensible gardening hours. Where no specific time for the change between phases is mentioned, this is because it happens early in the morning or late at night. For exact changeover times for any late-night or pre-dawn gardening, refer to the moon phase chart.

3rd quarter to new moon: 24th February–2nd and 25th–31st

A dormant period, with low sap and poor growth. Do not sow or plant. Prune, weed and harvest crops for storage. Fertilise and mulch the soil. Garden maintenance.

- Prune raspberries, red and white currants, and gooseberries.
- Weed and mulch beds. Pin polythene down to warm the soil.
- Protect cherry, apricot, peach and nectarine blossom from frosts. Plastic/glass coverings will protect peaches and nectarines from peach leaf curl.
- Feed perennials and overwintering plants – such as onions, kale, cabbages, hardy lettuces and leaves – with liquid feed.
- Feed and mulch fruit trees and bushes.
- Make a bean trench by digging out a trench and lining it with newspaper then filling it with compost and organic waste matter.

New moon to 1st quarter: 3rd–10th (till 10.45)

Rising vitality and upward growth. Plant and sow anything that develops above ground towards the end of the phase. Prepare for growth.

- Sow aubergines, chillies and peppers, cucumbers and tomatoes indoors in a heated propagator.

1st quarter to full moon: 10th (from 10.45)–17th
Sow crops that develop above ground, don't sow root crops. Plant out seedlings and young plants. Take cuttings and make grafts. Avoid other pruning. Fertilise.
- Sow aubergines, chillies and peppers, cucumbers and tomatoes indoors in a heated propagator.
- Sow Brussels sprouts, summer and autumn cabbages, celery, Florence fennel, lettuces and sprouting broccoli in pots or modules under cover.
- Sow hardy annual flower seeds.
- In mild areas and on light soils or pre-warmed ground, direct sow lettuces, peas, spinach and Swiss chard, and cover with cloches.
- Plant out broad beans and peas, under cloches.
- Gradually increase feeding and watering of houseplants.

Full moon to 3rd quarter: 18th–24th
A 'drawing down' energy. Sow and plant crops that develop below ground: root crops, bulbs and perennials.
- Plant onions sets, rhubarb crowns, asparagus crowns and Jerusalem artichokes.
- Plant new cold-stored strawberry runners and sow seeds of alpine strawberries.
- Lift, divide and replant perennial herbs.
- Chit seed potatoes. Start planting out first early potatoes.
- In mild areas and on light soils or pre-warmed ground, sow carrots, turnips, beetroot and radishes, and cover with cloches.
- Lift, split and replant crowded clumps of snowdrops.
- Plant lilies, dahlias and gladioli.
- Weed beds ahead of spring. Mulch them with organic matter. Prepare for planting out. Pinning clear or black polythene over beds will help warm the soil for early plantings.

THE KITCHEN

Lent this year begins on 2nd March. Traditionally this would have meant a very lean month of consuming no animal products and no sugar, a great national foray into veganism. Before that, though, there is pancake day, with the using up of milk and eggs and that last sprinkling of sugar. Other excuses for eating good things this month include several saints' days: David's, with Welsh cakes and rarebit; Patrick's, with Guinness cakes and soda breads; and Piran's, with pasties and cream teas. This is also the month when wild greens are at their best – get out into the woods and pick nettle tips and wild garlic.

In season

In the hedgerows, woods and fields
Wild greens: Alexanders, bistort, burdock, chickweed, comfrey leaves, dandelion, fat hen, Good-King-Henry, hawthorn tips, hop tips, nettle tips, orache, rampion, salad burnet, sea beet, sorrel, tansy, watercress, wild garlic, wintercress/yellow rocket, wood sorrel
Edible wild flowers: Primulas, cowslips, violets, gorse
Trees: Birch sap, cherry blossom
Game: Rabbit

From the seashore and rivers
Fish and shellfish: Oysters, scallops, mussels, elvers, coley, dab, lemon sole, cod, haddock, whiting, pollock, salmon
Seaweeds: Laver, kelp, pepper dulse, carragheen, egg wrack, sea lettuce, sugar kelp, sea kale

From the kitchen garden
Vegetables: Forced rhubarb, purple sprouting broccoli, Brussels sprouts, chicory, kale, onions, radishes, cabbages, cauliflowers, chard, endive, radicchio, lettuces, spinach, turnips, sorrel
Herbs: Winter savory, parsley, chervil, coriander, rosemary, bay, sage

From the farms
Fresh ewe's milk cheeses, Jersey Royal potatoes

RECIPES

Biscuit of the month

Cornish fairings

A biscuit to celebrate St Piran's Day on 5th March. St Piran is one of the patron saints of Cornwall, though St Petroc and St Michael also lay claim to it. This is a crunchy, chewy, spiced ginger biscuit originally sold at fairs and given by men to their sweethearts or to children as a treat.

Makes 12
Ingredients
4 tablespoons golden syrup
250g self-raising flour
3 teaspoons ground ginger
2 teaspoons mixed spice
1 teaspoon cinnamon
Pinch of salt
125g butter
125g golden caster sugar

Method

Preheat the oven to 200°C, Gas Mark 6. Line 2 baking sheets with nonstick baking paper. Warm the golden syrup by pouring it into a cup and sitting the cup in a shallow basin of just-boiled water. Sieve the flour and spices into a bowl and add the salt. Rub the butter into the flour mixture with your fingertips until it resembles breadcrumbs, then add the sugar and stir. Tip in the warmed syrup and stir in. Split the mixture into 12 pieces, and shape each piece into a ball. Place 6 balls on each baking sheet and bake for about 15 minutes, or until golden on top. Leave to cool on a wire rack.

Gorse flower and bay leaf liqueur

'When gorse is out of bloom, kissing is out of season,' the saying goes, because, of course, gorse blooms all year long. It is at its most floriferous in spring, though, and this would be a good time to pick some of these coconut and vanilla scented blooms for use in an infused liqueur. Bountiful they may be but gorse flowers are very tricky to pick, nestled as they are among vicious thorns, so wear gloves and take your time. Pick in the morning, taking nearly open buds rather than full-blown flowers. Check them for insects before using them.

Makes 1 litre

Ingredients
500g caster sugar
500ml water
1 litre gorse flowers
500ml vodka
4 bay leaves
Zest of 1 lemon

Method

Put the sugar and water into a pan and heat together until the sugar crystals dissolve and the syrup turns clear. Remove from the heat and leave to cool for 10 minutes. Put the gorse flowers into a large bowl or pan and pour the warm syrup over them. Cover and leave to infuse for 24 hours. Strain off the syrup and put it into a 1-litre jar with the vodka, bay leaves and lemon zest. Leave to infuse in a dark place for at least 1 month. Drink over ice, topped up with pineapple juice or sparkling water.

FOLK STORY OF THE MONTH

The Red Handkerchief

Here is a story that tells you all you need to know about leprechauns: how to discover where their gold is hidden, and how they will most probably get the better of you anyway.

A young man was walking along by moonlight when he heard a shriek. Being a fit and brave fellow, he ran to see what was afoot. Hanging from a blackthorn bush was a little man all dressed in green. At the base of the bush was a hammer and a pair of shoes. What luck! The man had found a leprechaun.

'What are you doing up there?' he said to the leprechaun.

'None of your business,' answered the leprechaun crossly. 'Just get me down!'

Now the man knew that as soon as he let go, the leprechaun would vanish, so he unhooked him but then kept a firm grip.

'Where is your pot of gold?' he demanded, looking the leprechaun firmly in the eye (because this is the way to make a leprechaun relinquish his treasure). The leprechaun sighed and pointed to another blackthorn bush.

While this was excellent news, our man couldn't dig it up with his bare hands. 'I will need to go and fetch my spade. How will I find the tree when I return?' he asked the leprechaun.

'I don't know and I don't care,' was the cross reply.

'Aha, I know! I will tie my red handkerchief to the tree and then I will be able to find it. But before I release you, you must promise that you will not touch it or move it while I am gone.'

'Yes, yes, I promise. Now let me go,' said the leprechaun.

And so the man let go of the leprechaun (who instantly vanished), tied his handkerchief to the tree and set off for home.

The next day he set off early to claim his fortune. He immediately spotted his tree, tied with the handkerchief, and started digging. But then he spotted another tree up ahead, also tied with a red handkerchief, and another, and another. In fact, every single blackthorn tree sported its own red handkerchief. The man knew then that the leprechaun had outwitted him, and he picked up his spade and headed for home.

NATURE

Bird of the month – skylark

This is a wonderful time to go out into the countryside and see if you can spot a skylark. Chances are, though, that you will hear one first, and when you see it the bird will be a mere speck, high above your head. Male skylarks rise vertically up into the air and then hover there, fluttering their wings to remain stationary. They stay at 50–200m high for up to an hour, singing their hearts out across the meadows, salt marshes, heath and farmland that they most often inhabit. The song is complex and varied, containing much mimicry of other birds – the songs of linnets, corn buntings, curlews and redshanks can all get thrown into the glorious mix, depending on the habitat that each skylark inhabits. Eventually they make a gliding, parachuting flight back down to the ground. Skylarks sing like this almost all year round. The song has different purposes throughout the year but in the spring it is to attract a mate.

Once they pair up, the skylarks go to the other extreme and make their cup-shaped grass nests directly on the ground. Sadly, these are very susceptible to predators, which may partly account for the extreme decline in the birds' numbers. Skylark pairs will lay several broods of eggs through the season. The hatchlings leave the nest before they can fly, after just eight to ten days, but they stay nearby and continue to be fed by the parents for a further ten days.

A little smaller than a starling, the skylark is an unremarkable-looking bird, with soft brown markings on the head and back and a pale brown breast, and the males and females are very similar. You are most likely to spot one by its behaviour and song. Larks have been much celebrated in poetry and music, and their song is traditionally associated with daybreak.

SKYLARK

M

FOLK SONG OF THE MONTH

'The Wearing of the Green'
Traditional, arr. Richard Barnard

This song charts a little of the history of the colour green, Ireland and St Patrick's Day. The Society of Irishmen, formed in the wake of the French Revolution to bring about an Irish national government with equal representation, adopted green as their colour. This is about the repression of those wearing it.

Oh, Paddy dear, and did you hear the news that's going round?
The shamrock is forbid by law to grow on Irish ground!
No more to keep Saint Patrick's Day, his colours can't be seen
For there's a cruel law against the Wearing of the Green.

Oh, I met with Napper Tandy and he took me by the hand
And he said, 'How's dear old Ireland and how does she stand?'
'She's the most distressful country that ever yet was seen,
For they're hanging men and women for the Wearing of the Green.'

And if the colour we must wear is England's cruel red
Let it remind us of the blood that Ireland has shed.
You may pull the shamrock from your hat and throw it on the sod
But you will see it take root there, though underfoot 'tis trod.

When laws can stop the blades of grass for growing as they grow
And when the leaves in summertime their colour dare not show
Then I will change the colour that I wear in my cáibín,
But 'til that day, please God, I'll stick to Wearing of the Green.

April

1 April Fools' Day

2 Ramadan begins, at sighting of the new moon (Muslim)

9 Grand National horse race

10 Palm Sunday (Christian)

14 St Tiburtius' Day – traditionally cuckoos sing from today (until St John's Day, 24th June)

15 Good Friday (Christian) – bank holiday, England, Wales, Scotland, Northern Ireland, Ireland

15 Passover/Pesach (Jewish) – begins at sundown, with the Seder feast

17 Easter Sunday (Christian)

18 Easter Monday (Christian) – bank holiday, England, Wales, Northern Ireland, Ireland

22 Orthodox Good Friday (Orthodox)

23 St George's Day – patron saint of England

23 Start of British asparagus season (ends at summer solstice, 21st June)

24 Orthodox Easter Sunday (Orthodox)

DRESSING UP IN APRIL

St George and the Pace Eggers

Eggs are a symbol of life and rebirth, and of springtime and Easter. The rural northern English tradition of Pace Egging – the word pace comes from *pascha*, the Latin word for Easter – saw 'Pace Eggers' or 'Jolly Boys' performing a mummers' play at local farms and large houses. It had a theme of death and resurrection, and the triumph of good over evil, in return for which the mummers were given eggs, beer and other food to make up an Easter feast. It may be one of many traditions that began life as Christmas mummers' plays intended to gather funds for Christmas celebrations but have gradually moved around the calendar over time, gaining the appropriate seasonal accoutrements.

The play does not have a particularly complex plot but it will include several characters from a wide potential number – including St George, the Noble Youth, the Lady Gay, Big Head, Slasher the Turkish Knight, the Soldier Brave, Lord Nelson and Betsy Brownbags. They fight, are slain and are then brought back to life by a farcical doctor with a magical cure. The delightfully named Old Toss Pot is another comedy character – despite getting laughs, he represents the devil. All in all, it is perhaps not the gentlest way of contemplating Christ's resurrection, but it apparently did the trick in medieval times.

The tradition has almost completely died out now but clings on (or more likely has been revived) in a few parts of Lancashire, including in Bury, where the Bury Pace Eggers tour local pubs over the Easter weekend. Their play revolves around St George fighting and slaying Slasher the Turkish Knight, who is then miraculously resurrected, with a clog dance by Big Head somewhere along the way. Money for charity is generally given now instead of eggs.

THE SKY

The evening sky is quiet for planets this month but we will see the very last of Venus before it vanishes into the glare of the rising sun. Mars has been at its dimmest through the beginning of the year but it will become increasingly visible until it reaches its brightest in December. We may get a first glimpse of it this month, and at the beginning of the month it will be alongside Saturn, which is about to reappear as a morning star.

At night

28th March–3rd April: The few days either side of the new moon are the best time to see 'earthshine', which is when the light shining onto the earth is reflected back onto the shadowy part of the moon. It is particularly pronounced in April and May and is also known as the 'ashen glow' or 'the old moon in the new moon's arms'.

5th: Close approach of Saturn and Mars. It will be difficult to see but possibly briefly visible around 05.30, low in the eastern sky.

By day

21st: At solar noon (approximately 13.00 BST/IST) the sun will reach an altitude of 50 degrees in the London sky and 46 degrees in the Glasgow sky.

1st–30th: Day length increases this month by 2h 4m at Clitheroe, Lancashire.

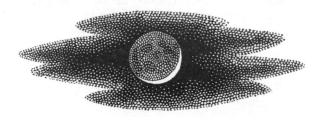

Sunrise and set
Clitheroe, Lancashire

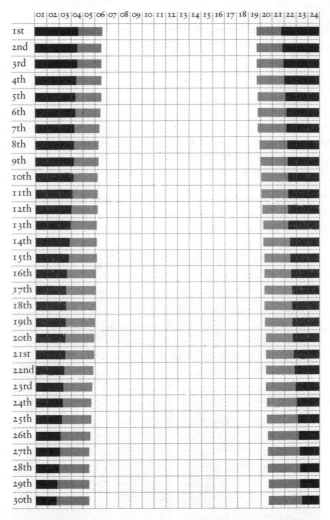

Deep-sky objects

Mizar and Alcor/Horse and Rider

For a long time Mizar and Alcor were thought to be twin stars, so close together as to have earned the name 'Horse and Rider'. Mizar makes up one of the corners of the Plough within Ursa Major. If you picture the Plough as a saucepan, Mizar is the star at the point where the handle kinks.

On closer inspection with telescopes, it has become apparent that Mizar and Alcor are, in fact, just the brightest stars in a six-star system. Mizar comprises two sets of binary stars, making it a quadruple star, and Alcor is a binary star. When you look at this corner of the Plough you are actually looking at a tiny star cluster. They are all thought to have the same origin, the same collapsing cloud of interstellar gas, and they are locked in orbit with each other. In fact, they share birth origins with several other stars in Ursa Major, the remains of a disintegrating star cluster, now widely scattered across the sky.

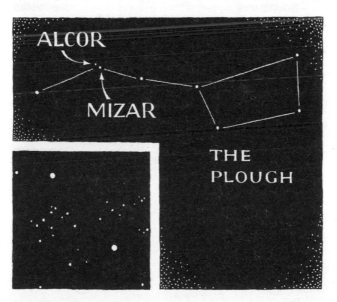

ALCOR

MIZAR

THE
PLOUGH

THE SEA

Average sea temperature

Shetland:	8.6°C
Greenock:	8.4°C
Cleethorpes:	8.1°C
Rhyl:	8.9°C
Rosslare:	9.5°C
Bideford:	9.7°C
Deal:	9.0°C

Spring and neap tides

Spring tides are the most extreme tides of the month, with the highest rises and the lowest falls, and they follow a couple of days after the full moon and new moon. Neap tides are the least extreme, with the smallest movement, and they fall in between the spring tides.

Spring tides: 3rd–5th and 18th–20th

Neap tides: 10th–11th and 24th–25th

Spring tides are shaded in black in the chart opposite.

April tide timetable for Dover

For guidance on how to convert this for your local area, see page 8.

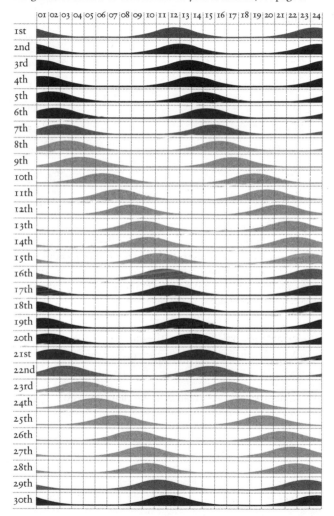

THE MOON

Moon phases

New moon – 1st April, 07.24

1st quarter – 9th April, 07.47

Full moon – 16th April, 19.55

3rd quarter – 23rd April, 12.56

New moon – 30th April, 21.28

Full moon

Names for April's full moon: Budding Moon, New Shoots Moon, Seed Moon.

This April's full moon is also the paschal full moon or ecclesiastical moon – the moon that determines the date of Easter. This is the name given to the first full moon on or after the vernal (spring) equinox, and then Easter is celebrated on the first Sunday after the paschal full moon. So, with the full moon on a Saturday this year, Easter is hard on its heels, on the 17th.

New moon

The first sighting of the crescent of the new moon on or around the 2nd will mark the beginning of the month of Ramadan, the month of fasting, and the holiest month in the Islamic year.

There are two new moons this April. Astrologers believe that the new moon is a good time to make plans, and that each new moon has a particular energy, depending on which zodiacal sign it is in. The first new moon, on the 1st, is in Aries, which is thought to pertain to creativity, fun and courage. The second, on the 30th, is in earthy Taurus, which makes it a good time to plan practical projects.

Moon phases for April

1st NEW	2nd	3rd	4th	5th
6th	7th	8th	9th	10th
11th	12th	13th	14th	15th
16th FULL	17th	18th	19th	20th
21st	22nd	23rd	24th	25th
26th	27th	28th	29th	30th NEW

A

THE GARDEN

Gardening by the moon

There is a huge amount to do this month, and a few risks do have to be taken with the still-fickle weather if you want to get your gardening underway ready for the burgeoning months of May and June. April is a lean month for harvesting – the 'hungry gap' – as winter and stored crops run out and new ones are yet to come in. An exception to this is glorious asparagus, the season for which starts on the 23rd – St George's Day.

Whether you are gardening in time with the moon or not, use the following as a guide to jobs to do in April.

Note: Sometimes these dates differ from those in the moon phase chart on page 81, to take into account sensible gardening hours. Where no specific time for the change between phases is mentioned, this is because it happens early in the morning or late at night. For exact changeover times for any late-night or pre-dawn gardening, refer to the moon phase chart.

New moon to 1st quarter: 1st–8th
Rising vitality and upward growth. Plant and sow anything that develops above ground towards the end of the phase. Prepare for growth.
- Sow any of the seeds in the 1st quarter to full moon phase towards the end of this period, or wait for the 1st quarter to full moon phase, which is even more suited to sowing. Prick out seedlings.
- Pot houseplants on and start watering them regularly and feeding them fortnightly.
- Prepare ground, mulch and feed soil.
- Remove covers from forced rhubarb. Feed perennials with liquid feed.
- Feed and mulch roses.

1st quarter to full moon: 9th–16th
Sow crops that develop above ground, don't sow root crops. Plant out seedlings and young plants. Take cuttings and make grafts. Avoid any other pruning. Fertilise.

- In pots under cover sow French beans, runner beans, cabbages, cauliflowers, courgettes, cucumbers, Florence fennel, kale, pumpkins and winter squashes, sweetcorn.
- This is your last chance to sow aubergines, chillies, peppers, melons and tomatoes indoors in a heated propagator.
- Start sowing herb seeds – coriander, chervil, dill, basil and parsley – in pots or seed trays indoors.
- Sow direct in warmer areas, but cover sowings with cloches: lettuces, peas, broad beans, rocket, summer purslane, corn salad, spinach and Swiss chard.
- Sow hardy flower seed in pots or direct. Sow sunflowers in pots.
- Plant up pots and hanging baskets with bedding plants but keep under cover until danger of frost has passed.

Full moon to 3rd quarter: 17th–23rd (till 12.56)
A 'drawing down' energy. Sow and plant crops that develop below ground: root crops, bulbs and perennials.
- Plant second early and maincrop potatoes.
- Sow direct in light soils in warm areas, covering with cloches after, for carrots, beetroot, parsnips, turnips, leeks, spring onions.
- Plant out asparagus crowns and globe artichokes, grapevines and strawberries.
- Plant lilies and gladioli.

3rd quarter to new moon: 23rd (from 12.56)–30th
A dormant period, with low sap and poor growth. Do not sow or plant. Prune, weed and harvest crops for storage. Fertilise and mulch the soil. Garden maintenance.
- Earth up first early potatoes.
- On warm days start to harden off plants that have been grown out-of-doors, moving them outside during the day and back in at night.
- Push shrubby peasticks into the ground to support peas. Build bamboo supports for French and runner beans.
- Weed and cut the lawn.

THE KITCHEN

This is the month that lemony sorrel and tender asparagus become available. There is green garlic, too, picked while fresh and mild and before it has matured enough to store. The Jersey potatoes start to arrive on the mainland, soft, tender and buttery. There are grander reasons for feasting, too: Lent ends midway through April, and weeks of frugality give way to Easter, with its abundance of chocolates, eggs and roast lamb, not to mention sweetened, spiced, yeasted breads – Italian Colomba di Pasqua, Greek *tsoureki*, Slovak *paska* and hot cross buns. Passover Seders take place this month too, with wine, matzo ball soup, gefilte fish, braised brisket and potato kugel.

In season

In the hedgerows, woods and fields
Wild greens: Alexanders, beech leaves, bistort, burdock, chickweed, comfrey leaves, dandelion, fat hen, Good-King-Henry, hawthorn tips, hop tips, nettle tips, orache, rampion, salad burnet, sea beet, sorrel, tansy, wintercress/yellow rocket, watercress, wild garlic, wood sorrel
Edible wild flowers: Cowslips, violets, broom, gorse

From the seashore and rivers
Fish and shellfish: Brown crab, sea trout, turbot, elvers, lobster, halibut, salmon, shrimp, whitebait
Seaweeds: Laver, pepper dulse, carragheen, eggwrack, sea lettuce, sugar kelp, sea kale

From the kitchen garden
Vegetables: Green garlic, asparagus, sorrel, purple sprouting broccoli, cauliflowers, chard, endive, lettuces, spring onions, radishes, spinach, turnips, cabbages, spring greens, rhubarb
Herbs: Parsley, chervil, coriander

From the farms
Fresh ewe's milk cheeses, Jersey Royal potatoes, asparagus

RECIPES

Biscuit of the month

Easter biscuits

In the West Country, this traditional shortcake-like biscuit is spiced with oil of cassia, a sweet, floral extract of cinnamon that was an ingredient of the anointing oil used on Jesus in the tomb. If you can't find it, you can use cinnamon.

Makes about 24
Ingredients
125g butter, softened
125g golden caster sugar, plus extra for sprinkling
1 egg
6 drops cassia oil (or ½ teaspoon ground cinnamon)
½ teaspoon mixed spice
Zest of 1 lemon
80g currants
300g plain flour
½ teaspoon baking powder
Pinch of salt
Freshly grated nutmeg, for sprinkling

Method

Line a baking sheet with nonstick baking paper. Cream the butter and the sugar together until soft and fluffy and then beat in the egg, cassia oil or cinnamon, mixed spice and lemon zest. Tip in the currants, flour, baking powder and salt, and mix it all into a soft, pliable dough. Roll out on a floured surface to 3mm thick and cut out rounds with a 5cm fluted biscuit cutter. Place on the lined baking sheet and refrigerate for 30 minutes. Preheat the oven to 180°C, Gas Mark 4 and bake for 12–15 minutes. They should still be pale and fairly soft in the centre and should break rather than snap. Immediately sprinkle with sugar and a grating of nutmeg. Leave to cool on a wire rack.

Carlin peas or parched peas

This is a traditional dish from northeast England, eaten on Passion Sunday, the Sunday before Palm Sunday, and so two weeks before Easter. The tradition is said to be linked to the siege of Newcastle in 1644, during England's First Civil War, when a French ship managed to dock and its cargo of dried peas saved the starving residents. Passion Sunday is still known as Carlin Sunday in many parts of northeast England. There is a northern saying to help remember the Sundays of lent: 'Tid, Mid, Miseray, Carlin, Palm, Pace Egg', with the first three referring to the hymns and psalms sung on those Sundays ('Te Deum Laudamus', 'Mi Deus' and 'Miserere Mei', respectively).

Serves 4

Ingredients

200g dried Carlin peas

1 teaspoon bicarbonate of soda (optional)

Large knob of butter

Malt vinegar

Salt and pepper

Method

Soak the peas in plenty of water overnight. Drain, change the water and bring to the boil, adding a teaspoon of bicarbonate of soda if you live in a hard water area. Boil hard for 10 minutes and then turn down the heat and simmer for about another 20 minutes. When the peas are soft, drain them. Melt a large knob of butter in a frying pan, add the peas and fry until the edges start to get crisp. Season with a little malt vinegar and salt and pepper, and serve. This dish is also traditional for Bonfire Night on 5th November, when they are served up around the bonfire in cones of paper.

Asparagus, anchovy soldiers and soft-boiled eggs

Who needs to make a fancy sauce for asparagus when soft-boiled eggs exist? This is a luxurious lunch to celebrate the start of the asparagus season. You can prepare the anchovy butter ahead of time and store it in the fridge.

A

Serves 2 as lunch or 4 as a snack
Ingredients
4 eggs
12 sticks asparagus, trimmed
4 slices bread

Anchovy butter
100g butter, softened
Leaves from a few sprigs of parsley, finely chopped
Zest of 1 lemon
6 anchovies, chopped finely
Salt and pepper

Method

Mix the anchovy butter ingredients together in a bowl. Put into a small ramekin and refrigerate if not using immediately. Now you need to boil the eggs, steam the asparagus and toast the bread at the same time. Bring water to a boil in a pan and more water to the boil in a steamer. Put the eggs into the pan and the asparagus into the top of the steamer. Boil the eggs for 5 minutes, then remove them and crack the tops to stop them cooking further; put them into egg cups. Remove the asparagus spears from the steamer after 5 minutes, and divide between the plates. Toast the bread on one side under a grill, then spread the anchovy butter on the other side and toast the buttered side under the grill. When it is browned and bubbling, remove the toast from the grill and cut it into strips ('soldiers'), then divide them among the plates. Serve.

Pace eggs

It has long been traditional to eat boiled eggs on Easter morning, after abstaining throughout Lent, and often they were decorated and given as gifts. You can use the traditional method to make your own beautiful marbled pace eggs.

Place a few well-shaped leaves or flowers on the raw eggs, then wrap them in onion skins, both red and white, and in spinach leaves and purple cabbage leaves. Wrap in aluminium foil and then lower into boiling water (water stained by beetroot or spinach is good, or use plain water) and boil for 7 minutes. Leave to cool completely in the water. When you unwrap them, they should be covered in swirls of colour, with the leaf and flower silhouettes retaining the original egg colour. Rub with a little butter to make them shiny, then display on the Easter breakfast table.

FOLK STORY OF THE MONTH

St George and the Dragon

The story of St George killing the dragon is a shining example of the mummers' tales of battles between the forces of good and the devil. It is, of course, also St George's Day on the 23rd April. History tells us that St George never even set foot in England and that the following story was originally set in Cappadocia (modern Turkey), but legend still insists it all happened on Dragon Hill at Uffington in Oxfordshire. The flat top of this hillock has a patch where grass will not grow, the blood of the dragon being so poisonous that it still kills the grass all of these hundreds of years later.

There was once a town plagued by a dragon that ravaged the countryside, poisoning the fields and eating the livestock. The townspeople were distraught, so they offered the dragon sacrifices. At first these were two sheep, each day; then a man and a sheep; and finally the youths of the town, drawn by lot and sent to die. One day this fate fell to the king's daughter. The king offered the people all of his money to save her, but the people insisted that what was good enough for their children was good enough for her. The king's daughter was dressed as a bride and walked in a procession down to the dragon's lair.

St George was at that moment nearby, and when he saw the girl and heard the tale he vowed to protect her. When the dragon emerged to claim its meal, St George made the sign of the cross at it and then charged on his horse, wounding the dragon with his lance. St George shouted to the princess to throw him her girdle, and he then placed this around the dragon's neck, at which the dragon suddenly became calm and meekly followed them back into the town.

St George offered to slay the dragon if the townspeople converted to Christianity and were baptised, and surprisingly enough they agreed. He beheaded it with his sword and the townspeople were able to live in peace.

SONG OF THE MONTH

'Pace Egging Song'
Traditional, arr. Richard Barnard

This song is thought to originate in Lancashire, which makes
sense as this is where the tradition of Pace Egging has always
been strongest and where it has clung on longest. The song
mentions many of the characters that turn up in the play, and
is a bit silly all round.

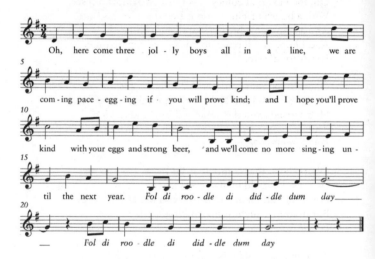

Oh, here come three jolly boys all in a line,
We are coming pace-egging if you will prove kind;
And I hope you'll prove kind with your eggs and strong
beer,
And we'll come no more singing until the next year.
Fol-di-roodle di diddle dum day
Fol-di-roodle di diddle dum day

Oh, the next that comes in is Lord Nelson, you'll see,
With a bunch of blue ribbons tied down to his knee,
And a star on his breast, like silver it shines
And I hope you'll remember it's pace-egging time.
Fol-di-roodle etc.

Oh, the next that comes in is a jolly Jack Tar,
He sailed with Lord Nelson all through the last war.
He's arrived from the ocean old England to view
And he's come a-pace-egging with our jovial crew.
Fol-di-roodle etc.

Oh, the next that comes in is Old Toss Pot you see,
He's a valiant old man in every degree;
He's a valiant man, and he wears a pig-tail,
But his only delight is in drinking mulled ale.
Fol-di-roodle etc.

Then in comes old miser all with her brown bags,
For fear of her money she wears her old rags.
So, mind what you do and see that all's right;
If you give nought, we'll take nought, farewell and good
night!
Fol-di-roodle etc.

NATURE

Bird of the month – cuckoo

There is a huge amount of superstition and folklore surrounding Cuckoo Day and the first cuckoo call of the year, which is said to occur on the 14th April, or the 15th, or the 20th, depending on where you are (Sussex, Northamptonshire and Worcestershire, respectively). The number of calls you hear that first time will determine how many years you have left to live, or perhaps how many before you marry. It is most important that it is off to your right, and you certainly don't want to hear it from your left or behind you. Lucky you if you have some coins in your pocket when you hear it and luckier still if you jingle them – you will have no money worries for the coming year. Tough luck if you hear it from your bed, as you have an illness upcoming unless you leap up immediately and start running. Good stuff if you are standing on grass as you hear it, but woe betide you if you are standing on stone.

As well as cuckoos being heralds of spring, it is surely their brutal breeding habits that have made them such creatures of fascination. The striped underside mimics the sparrowhawk, sending little birds scattering for cover, and giving the female time to lay her egg in their nest. It hatches after just 12 days and pushes any other eggs or hatchlings out of the nest, and is then fed by its adopted parents for a full month. The hatchling grows quickly and has a huge appetite – often growing to several times the size of its adopted and increasingly exhausted and bedraggled parents while still demanding they feed it. A female cuckoo may visit and lay an egg in up to 50 nests in a breeding season.

By September both the adults and their chicks will mostly have flown to the Central and West African savannah and rainforest where they will spend the winter, resting and gaining strength in preparation for wreaking havoc on little birds and on those with a superstitious turn of mind.

CUCKOO

A

May

- **1** May Day (traditional)
- **1** Beltane (Gaelic/pagan/neopagan)
- **1** International Workers' Day
- **1** International Dawn Chorus Day
- **2** Early May bank holiday, England, Wales, Scotland, Northern Ireland
- **2** May Day bank holiday, Ireland
- **2** 2nd–3rd: Eid al-Fitr – celebration of the end of Ramadan, at the sighting of the new moon (Muslim)
- **12** Stowe Horse Fair – spring Gypsy, Romani and Traveller gathering
- **22** Rogation Sunday/beating the bounds (Christian/traditional)
- **26** Ascension Day, Holy Thursday (Christian)

DRESSING UP IN MAY

Robin Hood and the Green Man

The Green Man is the spirit of summer, the Oak King to winter's Holly King (see page 12), picking up the reins as summer begins, or even fighting and killing the Holly King to allow the summer in. In some May celebrations he will appear as Jack-in-the-Green, Puck or Robin Goodfellow. But he is Robin Hood at Helston, in Cornwall, at the Hal-an-Tow, which is part of the Flora Day celebrations (usually held on 8th May, unless that is a Sunday or Monday, in which case it is held on the previous Saturday).

Some scholars have assumed that Robin Hood was a real human being, while others have put his legendary status down to something more pagan and supernatural: a summer lord and king of the greenwood, an outlaw spirit and a virile symbol of the growth, fertility and careless pleasure of the summer. Although it seems likely that he was a real woodland rebel, over the centuries he has blended into a combination of the two.

What we do know for certain is that Robin Hood was the subject of several ballads, which later were turned into plays that became central to early Tudor May Games, presumably due to the joy to be had hearing about an outlaw outwitting an oppressive ruling class. May Games occurred each year during the slight breathing space between the major agricultural jobs of early spring (ploughing and sowing) and summer (haymaking). Over time, such plays morphed into Morris Dances, and Robin Hood vanished from them, while other characters including Maid Marian remained.

But Robin Hood survives in the Hal-an-Tow. This is a mystery play and pageant revived from an earlier celebration, thought to once have been widespread through Cornwall and rural areas elsewhere. It sets off early in the morning of Flora Day and makes its way around Helston. Its characters include Spanish sailors, St Piran, St George and the dragon, St Michael and the devil, and Robin Hood with his Merry Men. The song 'Hal-an-Tow' is sung and the verses acted out, all surrounded by a ring of people bedecked in greenery and spring flowers, determined to welcome the summer in raucous fashion.

THE SKY

This month will see a total lunar eclipse, as the earth slips directly between the sun and the moon, casting its shadow on the moon, though unfortunately it will be tricky to see because of its timing. Jupiter appears in our skies this month for the first time since February, rising in the east at about 03.00 before being lost in the dawn an hour or so later. It will gradually get higher and brighter throughout the year.

At night

28th April–3rd May: The few days either side of the new moon are the best time to see 'earthshine', which is when the light shining onto the earth is reflected back onto the shadowy part of the moon. It is particularly pronounced in April and May and is known as the 'ashen glow' or 'the old moon in the new moon's arms'.

16th: Total lunar eclipse. Totality at 04.30. This eclipse will be difficult to see as the moon will be close to the horizon and setting. The shadow of the earth will touch it at 03.30 when it is at 11 degrees. By 04.30, when it is in total shadow, it should be darkish red in colour but will be at just 5 degrees from the horizon and will start to get lost in the dawn around this time. Land's End will get an extra 20 minutes.

By day

21st: At solar noon (approximately 13.00 BST/IST) the sun will reach an altitude of 59 degrees in the London sky and 55 degrees in the Glasgow sky.

1st–31st: Day length increases this month by 1h 40m at Clitheroe, Lancashire.

Sunrise and set
Clitheroe, Lancashire

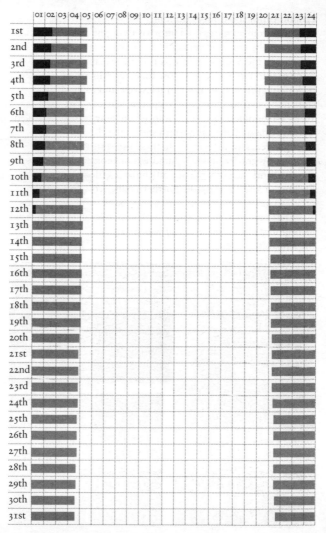

Deep-sky objects

Epsilon Lyrae/the Double Double

Epsilon Lyrae, in the constellation of Lyra, the Harp, is
known as the Double Double. To the naked eye it looks like
any star in the sky, but train a pair of binoculars on it and it
resolves into two stars, very close together. Magnify further
by looking through an amateur telescope and each of these
stars resolves into another two separate stars. In fact, in the
1980s astronomers using an advanced imaging technique called
'speckle imaging' detected a fifth star in the cluster. About
162 light years away from earth, these five stars are bound
together by gravity, and take hundreds of thousands of years to
orbit around each other. The pairs move a little more quickly:
Epsilon 1a and 1b, the more northern pair, orbit around each
other over 1,800 years; Epsilon 2a and 2b take about 724 years.

   The constellation of Lyra is high in the sky in summer. Find
its brightest star, Vega, and you will see Epsilon Lyrae just to
the left of it.

M

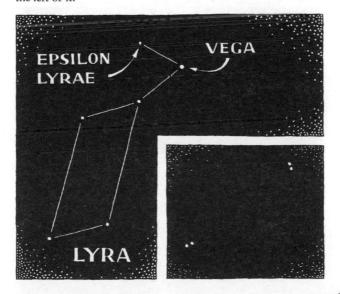

THE SEA

Average sea temperature

Shetland:	9.6°C
Greenock:	9.8°C
Cleethorpes:	9.9°C
Rhyl:	10.9°C
Rosslare:	10.9°C
Bideford:	11.5°C
Deal:	11.4°C

Spring and neap tides

Spring tides are the most extreme tides of the month, with the highest rises and the lowest falls, and they follow a couple of days after the full moon and new moon. Neap tides are the least extreme, with the smallest movement, and they fall in between the spring tides.

Spring tides: 1st–3rd, 17th–19th and 31st–2nd June

Neap tides: 9th–10th and 23rd–25th

Spring tides are shaded in black in the chart opposite.

May tide timetable for Dover

For guidance on how to convert this for your local area, see page 8.

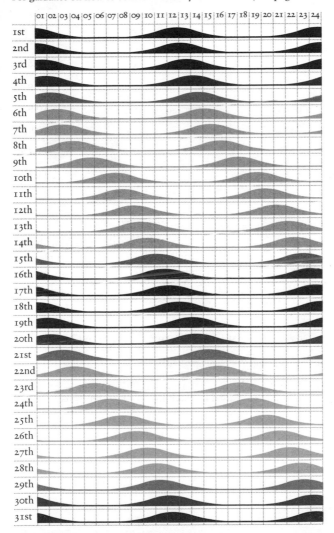

	01	02	03	04	05	06	07	08	09	10	11	12	13	14	15	16	17	18	19	20	21	22	23	24

1st
2nd
3rd
4th
5th
6th
7th
8th
9th
10th
11th
12th
13th
14th
15th
16th
17th
18th
19th
20th
21st
22nd
23rd
24th
25th
26th
27th
28th
29th
30th
31st

THE MOON

Moon phases

1st quarter – 9th May, 01.21

Full moon – 16th May, 05.14

3rd quarter – 22nd May, 19.43

New moon – 30th May, 12.30

Full moon

Names for May's full moon: Mother's Moon, Bright Moon.
There will be a total eclipse of the full moon this month.

New moon

The first sighting of the crescent moon is expected at sundown on 2nd May. This will signal the end of the Islamic holy month of Ramadan and the beginning of Eid al-Fitr, the Festival of Breaking the Fast.

This month's new moon on 30th May is in Gemini. Astrologers believe that the new moon is a good time to make plans and focus on your dreams and hopes for the period ahead, and that each new moon has a particular energy, depending on which zodiacal sign it is in. Gemini governs communication, making this a good time to plan projects involving dialogue, broadcasting and making connections.

Moon phases for May

1st	2nd	3rd	4th	5th
6th	7th	8th	9th	10th
11th	12th	13th	14th	15th
16th FULL	17th	18th	19th	20th
21st	22nd	23rd	24th	25th
26th	27th	28th	29th	30th NEW
31st				

M

THE GARDEN

Gardening by the moon

The weather is warming, growth is leaping, and we are itching to plant out seedlings. Do beware, though, of the 'Ice Saints' – St Mamertus, St Pancras and St Servatius – whose feast days fall on the 11th, 12th and 13th May respectively. They sometimes herald a 'blackthorn winter', a cold snap that can bring the final frosts of spring. Keep horticultural fleece handy, and watch the weather forecast. Once past the Ice Saints, we are generally in the clear – the end of May will be a frenzy of planting out.

Whether you are gardening in time with the moon or not, use the following as a guide to jobs to do in May.

Note: Sometimes these dates differ from those in the moon phase chart on page 103, to take into account sensible gardening hours. Where no specific time for the change between phases is mentioned, this is because it happens early in the morning or late at night. For exact changeover times for any late-night or pre-dawn gardening, refer to the moon phase chart.

New moon to 1st quarter: 1st–8th and 30th (from 12.30)–7th June (till 15.48)

Rising vitality and upward growth. Plant and sow anything that develops above ground towards the end of the phase. Prepare for growth.

- All of the seed sowing in the next phase can be done now, particularly towards the end of this phase, though the next phase is more conducive.
- Plant out vegetable plants, including tender plants such as tomatoes and winter squashes, and put out hanging baskets and bedding towards the end of the month, or once you are confident that the last frosts have passed.
- Pot chillies and tomatoes into their final pots.

1st quarter to full moon: 9th–15th

Sow crops that develop above ground, don't sow root crops.

Plant out seedlings and young plants. Take cuttings and make grafts. Avoid other pruning. Fertilise.

- Direct sow corn salad, French beans, runner beans, sweetcorn, Brussels sprouts, calabrese, cauliflowers, Florence fennel, kale, lettuces, peas, spinach and purple sprouting broccoli, plus cucumbers under cloches. Sow coriander, chervil, dill and parsley direct under cloches. Sow basil in pots indoors.
- Sow Brussels sprouts and broccoli in a temporary seedbed or in pots. Start courgettes, pumpkins and squashes in pots indoors.
- Plant out vegetable plants, including tender plants such as tomatoes and winter squashes, and put out hanging baskets and bedding towards the end of the month, or once you are confident that the last frosts have passed.

Full moon to 3rd quarter: 16th–22nd
A 'drawing down' energy. Sow and plant crops that develop below ground: root crops, bulbs and perennials.
- Lift, split and replant overcrowded clumps of spring bulbs and spring-flowering perennials.
- Direct sow beetroot, carrots, kohlrabi, radishes, spring onions, swedes and turnips.
- Plant lilies, dahlias and gladioli.

3rd quarter to new moon: 23rd–30th (till 12.30)
A dormant period, with low sap and poor growth. Do not sow or plant. Prune, weed and harvest crops for storage. Fertilise and mulch. Garden maintenance.
- Earth up potatoes.
- Weed.
- Prune spring-flowering clematis.
- Tie in climbers and ramblers.
- Liquid feed spring bulbs that have finished flowering.
- Put supports in place for herbaceous perennials.
- Tie in sweet peas as they grow.
- Net fruit bushes.

THE KITCHEN

Late May turns us all into foragers as the hedgerows explode with sweet-scented elderflower in great clouds of creamy white. Gather bagfuls and take them back to the kitchen to make your elderflower champagne for drinking as summer days lengthen. There are also the anise-scented flowers of sweet cicely to pluck, and a great flush of wild edible leaves at their freshest and greenest: Good-King-Henry, wood sorrel and watercress. The pickings in the vegetable garden are still fairly lean this month, but we might see the first mouth-puckeringly sour gooseberries and some early strawberries if we are lucky. And they are not the only fruit: Alphonso mango season is here, so get hold of some of these most fragrant and succulent of mangoes while their brief season lasts. They will be gone by the end of June.

In season

In the hedgerows, woods and fields
Wild greens: Alexanders, beech leaves, bistort, burdock, chickweed, comfrey leaves, dandelion, fat hen, Good-King-Henry, hawthorn tips, hop tips, nettle tips, orache, rampion, salad burnet, sea beet, sorrel, tansy, wintercress/yellow rocket, watercress, wood sorrel
Wild herbs: Cleavers, hairy bittercress, hedge garlic, lemon balm, wild marjoram, spearmint, sweet cicely, wild thyme, wild fennel
Edible wild flowers: Elderflowers, sweet cicely, broom, borage, chamomile, hawthorn, marigolds, pansies, violets, wild roses
Wild fruits: Wild gooseberries

From the seashore and rivers
Fish and shellfish: Herring, brown crab, lobster, sea trout, turbot, sardine, plaice, sea bass, mackerel, salmon
Seaweeds: Laver, pepper dulse, carragheen, eggwrack, sea lettuce, sugar kelp

From the kitchen garden
Vegetables: Asparagus, broad beans, baby globe artichokes, peas, radishes, wild rocket, beetroot, hispi cabbages, cauliflowers, chard, endive, green garlic, lettuces, spring onions, spinach, spring greens, turnips, sorrel
Herbs: Chives and chive flowers, parsley, chervil

From the farms
Cheddar Valley strawberries, ewe's milk cheeses and goat curds, ricotta, Stinking Bishop, garlic yarg, Jersey Royal potatoes, Cornish and Ayrshire earlies, asparagus, spring lamb

And traditional imports
Alphonso mango

M

RECIPES

Biscuit of the month

Bülbül yuvasi baklava – nightingale's nests

Admittedly, baklava is not quite a biscuit, or it's a very luxurious and sticky biscuit if it is, but baklava and coffee are definitely the Turkish equivalent of tea and biscuits. It is included to celebrate the arrival and song of the nightingales.

Makes 6
Ingredients
Syrup
170g caster sugar
130ml water
Juice of ½ lemon
1 teaspoon orange flower water
Pastry
6 sheets filo pastry
110g butter, melted
150g finely chopped almonds, walnuts or pistachios
18 whole blanched almonds

Method

Make the syrup by combining the sugar and water in a pan and heating it until it clears. Add the lemon juice and boil until it reaches 106°C on a sugar thermometer and turns thick and syrupy. Remove from the heat and add the flower water. Leave to cool.

Preheat the oven to 180°C, Gas Mark 4. Lay a filo sheet on your work surface, and place the others under a damp tea towel to stop them from drying out. Brush the filo sheet all over with butter and scatter 20g chopped nuts over the whole surface except for a 5cm band at the top end.

Roll it up as tightly as you can from the bottom end, creating a cigar shape. When you reach the final 5cm, push sections of it inward all along its length to make it shorter and to create a ruffled and nest-like texture. Twist the ends so that they meet, forming a nest shape, with the bare 5cm forming the base. Place the nest on a 20 x 25cm baking sheet with a lip, then brush all over the nest with butter.

Repeat for the remaining filo sheets, placing the nests snugly up against each other to hold them in place. Use the remaining 30g of chopped nuts to put a little 'rubble' in the bottom of each nest. Top with three blanched almonds per nest, and brush with melted butter again.

Bake for 30 minutes or until golden brown. Remove from the oven and pour the syrup over the nests immediately, then cover with foil and leave to cool completely before eating.

M

Elderflower *sima* – elderflower mead

Sima is Finnish spring mead, a lightly fermented, honey-based lemonade that is traditionally drunk on May Day. The goal is to ferment it just enough to create a light fizz. It does not traditionally contain elderflowers and you can certainly make it without, but they are a gorgeous addition, adding their floral, honey flavours to this most summery of drinks.

Makes 1.1 litres
Ingredients
120ml runny honey
1 lemon, thinly sliced
5 raisins
1 litre water
3 heads of elderflower (optional)
Pinch of wine yeast

Method

Put the honey, lemon and raisins into a large bowl. Boil the water, pour it over and stir. Ten minutes later add the elderflower. Cover the bowl with a tea towel and leave for a couple of hours, then fish out and discard the flower heads. Add the pinch of yeast and stir well. Decant into a 1.1 litre preserving jar and cover with a piece of muslin, tying the muslin in place. Allow to ferment at room temperature. After 1–2 days the raisins will float to the top, which is a sign that the *sima* is ready. Strain the liquid into a clean preserving jar or into screw-top or flip-top bottles and store in the refrigerator for a further few days to increase carbonation if you like, opening the bottles once a day to release pressure. Drink within 1 week.

Tippaleipä – funnel cakes for May Day

This is a Finnish recipe traditionally served as part of May Day celebrations, along with a drink of *sima* (see opposite).

Makes about 20
Ingredients
Vegetable or sunflower oil, for frying
7 egg whites and 1 whole egg
160g caster sugar
175g plain flour
Icing sugar, for dusting

M

Method
Pour the oil into a heavy-bottomed pot so it is one-third full. Whisk the egg whites, whole egg and sugar together until they are foamy, then sift in the flour and fold it in. Fill an uncut piping bag with the batter and use a bag clip to hold it closed. You will need a second clip for after you have snipped the end – or one person can look after the job of pouring and another the job of flipping and lifting from the oil. (Alternatively, a large squeezy catering ketchup bottle would be ideal.)

Heat the oil to 170°–180°C on a sugar thermometer, or when a cube of bread dropped into the oil turns brown in around 30 seconds. Snip a very small hole in the end of the piping bag, and drizzle a swirling criss-crossing shape into the hot oil. At first it will seem as if it is just going to disperse across the pan, but persevere with swirling and criss-crossing in the same spot, and the batter will soon join together.

Clip the end of the piping bag closed, and move it over the pan to make another cake, clipping the end of it while they are cooking. (Once you have practised a few times you might be able to manage three in the pan at a time, but note that they only need a minute or so of frying on each side.) Flip them over and cook on the second side until they are browned all over, and then lift them from the oil and drain on kitchen paper. Sift icing sugar over them and eat as soon as they are cool enough.

NATURE

Bird of the month – nightingale

Nightingales are plain little birds with beautiful voices, perhaps the most rich, varied and melodic of all of the birds: a great crystalline holding forth of trills, churrs, buzzes, whistles and crescendos. They have a vast range of over a thousand different sounds to call upon, compared with the blackbird's hundred. More magical still is that they start to sing as dusk falls, and carry on singing well into the night.

In Britain, nightingales are mainly found in the southeast of England and are scarce even there, having declined by 90 per cent in the last 50 years due to habitat changes. There are thought to be no more that 5,000–6,000 singing males left. If you find yourself in one of their chosen spots, they are a great deal easier to hear than to see. Their appearance is nondescript to say the least – small, brown, a little like a slightly larger robin without the splash of colour – and they often hide away in impenetrable scrub.

It is the male birds that sing through the night, hoping to attract the attention of a female bird as she flies above. Males make their migration a little before females, setting up and defending their territories ready for the females' arrival. Each male will perch high up in a tree in his territory and sing between late April and early June, and the females will fly between the males, listening and moving on until they find a song that is to their liking. Once a male has caught the attention of a female, he will continue courting her with snatches of song sung at a quieter volume, and dropping the whistles from his repertoire, which are perhaps there to beckon the female towards him.

The male and female raise their chicks together. It is thought that the complexity of the male's song is partly an advertisement of how experienced a father he is – he picks up new patterns and trills each year – and how good he will be at helping her raise the chicks. Some poor males sadly do not make the grade, and will continue singing on through the night until late July, when it is time to leave for Africa.

NIGHTINGALE

FOLK STORY OF THE MONTH

Robin Hood and the Potter

This story was often acted out during the May Games, which traditionally consisted of the election of a May king and queen; a procession when the Hal-an-Tow song was performed; a Morris dance and a hobby horse dance; and a Robin Hood play. The story is typical of tales of Robin Hood, courting trouble with authority, generous to a fault and popular with the ladies.

One day in early summer, when the leaves were springing and there were blossoms on every bough, Robin Hood and his Merry Men saw a potter with a cart of pots coming through the forest. Little John, Robin's right-hand man, had met the man before in a fight, and he bet Robin that he would never be able to take a payment from him for passing by. Robin challenged the man and the two fought, the potter squarely beating Robin. Admitting defeat, Robin said, 'Let's have a little fun. You give me your clothes and I will give you mine, and I will go as you to Nottingham and sell your pots.' The potter agreed, and Little John warned Robin to avoid the Sheriff of Nottingham, who was a great enemy.

When he arrived in Nottingham, Robin – disguised as the potter – set up his stall and started crying, 'Pots! Great bargains!' and all of the women gathered around, whispering that he must be very new to making pots, to sell them so cheaply. When nearly all the pots were sold, Robin sent the last five to the wife of the Sheriff of Nottingham, who came to thank him and – taking a liking to him – invited him to dine with her and her husband. As they ate, two of the Sheriff's men talked of an upcoming shooting match, and Robin asked to join in. He easily beat the men, astonishing the Sheriff, so Robin told him that he had learned his skills shooting 100 bouts with Robin Hood, and that he would lead the Sheriff to him if he wished. Delighted, the sheriff promised to reward him handsomely once Robin was captured.

When they were deep in the woods, Robin said, 'By my horn we shall find out if Robin Hood is nearby', and he blew a great blast. Soon the Merry Men arrived and robbed the Sheriff of his horse and the reward, sending him home by foot. 'If it weren't for the love of your dear wife,' said Robin, 'you would see much more trouble. The woman is very good.' And he told the Sheriff that he would be sending her a gift of a palfrey, a small, delicate horse popular among noblewomen. When the Sheriff finally got home and told his wife the tale, she laughed at him and said that at least now he had paid for the pots.

Robin returned to the greenwood tree, paid the potter ten pounds to cover the price of the pots, and told him that he was welcome to pass through the forest at any time.

SONG OF THE MONTH

'Hal-an-Tow'
Traditional, arr. Richard Barnard

This is sung during the Hal-an-Tow procession around
Helston on Flora Day (see page 96). It mentions Robin Hood
and Little John and may be a remnant of earlier May Games
(see pages 96 and 114) that featured Robin Hood tales.

Hal-an-Tow! Jolly Rumble-O!
For we are up as soon as any day-O,
And for to fetch the summer home,
The summer and the May-O;
The summer is a come-O
And winter is a gone-O.

Robin Hood and Little John,
They both are gone to fair-o,
And we go to the green wood
To see what they do there-o;
And for to chase-o,
To chase the buck and doe.

Hal-an-Tow! etc.

Where are those Spaniards
That make so great a boast-o?
For they shall eat the grey goose feather
And we will eat the roast-o
In every land-o
The land that e'er we go.

Hal-an-Tow! etc.

As for that brave knight, St George
St George he was a knight-o.
Of all the knights in Christendom,
King George he is the right-o
In every land-o
The land that e'er we go.

Hal-an-Tow! etc.

June

1 Start of meteorological summer

1 Start of Pride Month

1 Start of Gypsy, Roma and Traveller History Month

2 Spring bank holiday, England, Wales, Scotland, Northern Ireland

2 2nd–5th: Appleby Horse Fair, Cumbria – Gypsy, Roma and Traveller gathering

3 Platinum Jubilee bank holiday, England, Wales, Scotland, Northern Ireland

4 4th–6th: Feast of Weeks/Shavuot, begins at sundown (Jewish)

5 Whit Sunday/Pentecost (Christian)

6 June bank holiday, Ireland

19 Father's Day

21 Summer solstice – start of astronomical summer

21 Litha (pagan, neopagan)

21 World Humanist Day

24 Midsummer Day (traditional)

24 Feast of St John the Baptist (Christian)

DRESSING UP IN JUNE

Summer solstice at Stonehenge

The summer solstice falls on 21st June this year, when
thousands of people gather at Stonehenge to watch the sun
rising just to the left of the Heel Stone. (It is thought that there
was once a second stone, and the sun would have been framed
between it and the Heel Stone.) The historical basis for this
is a little hazy. The exact ways in which people from the late
Neolithic onwards made use of Stonehenge are fiercely debated,
but it seems to have always been a place of gathering and ritual,
and we know that those gatherings were centred around the
solstices and the equinoxes. Stonehenge works as a great stone
almanac of the year, the sun falling through particular slots
between stones on the key dates.

Although it seems likely that the winter solstice saw the
largest gatherings in ancient times, it is the summer solstice
that now draws the greatest crowd, with up to ten thousand
attendees. The only formalised dress for the event is the long
white robe, the attire of the modern-day druids, for whom
this is a religious occasion. Their ceremony is joyful and full
of music and poetry, and includes – of course – a mock fight
between the Holly King and the Oak King (see page 96).

But the wider event is also host to a great creative flowering
of interpretations of British folklore and mythology. Folkloric,
pagan and mythical figures from around the year appear – the
Green Man, the Mari Lwyd (a Welsh traditional folk costume
made from a horse's skull), Maid Marian, Merlin, King Arthur,
pagan goddesses, witches and wizards, horned men, unicorns,
Morris dancers and the Nordic sun goddess Sunna. It is a great
mash-up of anything and everything that may or may not
reside in Britain's pagan past, with a few Aztecs and Native
Americans thrown in for good measure. Perhaps the latter
reflects a longing for the connection with the land and nature
that is associated with indigenous cultures, and which many
seek in Britain's lost paganism. Summer solstice at Stonehenge
has become a great gathering of those who want to celebrate
the turning of the seasons, and who wish to celebrate our
pagan past, mysterious as it may be.

THE SKY

June brings with it the summer solstice, the longest day and shortest night of the year. There will also be a super full moon, and Jupiter will be around in the later part of the same night, from midnight until around 04.00 very low in the southern sky. There is a chance to see a conjunction of Jupiter alongside the waning moon later in the month.

At night

14th: Super full moon. This occurs when the point at which the moon is closest to the earth in its elliptical orbit coincides with a full moon. It can look up to 14 per cent bigger and 30 per cent brighter than a micromoon, which is when its furthest-away point coincides with a full moon.

21st: Jupiter and the moon rise together at 01.40 in the east. They will become lost in the dawn at 04.00 in the southeast, while at an altitude of 23 degrees.

By day

21st: The summer solstice falls at 10.13, the moment that the sun is directly overhead at the Tropic of Cancer, the northernmost latitude at which it can be directly overhead. The word solstice comes from the Latin *solstitium*, meaning 'sun stopping', and is related to the position of sunrise and sunset on the horizon. Both positions have been moving north day by day and will now pause for a while, then start to head south.

21st: At solar noon (approximately 13.00 BST/IST) the sun will reach an altitude of 62 degrees in the London sky and 58 degrees in the Glasgow sky.

1st–30th: Day length increases this month by 24m up to the solstice on the 21st, and then decreases by 4m by the end of the month, in Clitheroe, Lancashire.

Sunrise and set
Clitheroe, Lancashire

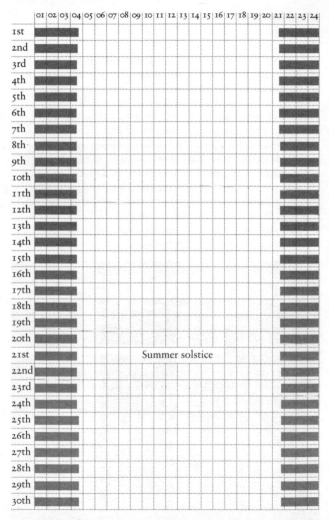

	01	02	03	04	05	06	07	08	09	10	11	12	13	14	15	16	17	18	19	20	21	22	23	24
1st																								
2nd																								
3rd																								
4th																								
5th																								
6th																								
7th																								
8th																								
9th																								
10th																								
11th																								
12th																								
13th																								
14th																								
15th																								
16th																								
17th																								
18th																								
19th																								
20th																								
21st						Summer solstice																		
22nd																								
23rd																								
24th																								
25th																								
26th																								
27th																								
28th																								
29th																								
30th																								

Deep-sky objects

The Milky Way

In June the Milky Way rises just after sunset and under dark skies is visible all night long. The Milky Way is the name of our galaxy, a celestial pinwheel with numerous 'arms' spinning off it, 100,000 light years across. In fact, every single star that we can see in the sky is within it. But in terms of stargazing, when we talk about the Milky Way we are referring to the luminous band made up of millions upon millions of stars so distant and numerous that they blend into a hazy river punctuated by star clusters and nebulae. This is what we can see of our galaxy as we look along its flat plane from our point on one of the spiral's minor arms (the Orion Arm). In the summer months we are facing the galaxy's bright centre, a shining bulge of around ten billion stars. Our view is partially obscured by vast clouds of interstellar dust – without this, the light reaching us from the galaxy's core on summer nights would be strong enough to cast shadows.

THE
MILKY WAY

THE SEA

Average sea temperature

Shetland:	11.2°C
Greenock:	11.7°C
Cleethorpes:	12.8°C
Rhyl:	13.3°C
Rosslare:	12.8°C
Bideford:	13.9°C
Deal:	14.2°C

Spring and neap tides

Spring tides are the most extreme tides of the month, with the highest rises and the lowest falls, and they follow a couple of days after the full moon and new moon. Neap tides are the least extreme, with the smallest movement, and they fall in between the spring tides.

Spring tides: 1st–2nd and 15th–17th

Neap tides: 8th–9th and 22nd–23rd

Spring tides are shaded in black in the chart opposite.

June tide timetable for Dover

For guidance on how to convert this for your local area, see page 8.

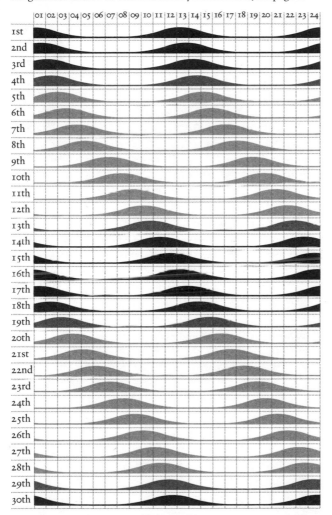

J

THE MOON

Moon phases

1st quarter – 7th June, 15.48	
Full moon – 14th June, 12.51	
3rd quarter – 21st June, 04.10	
New moon – 29th June, 03.52	

Full moon

Names for June's full moon: Rose Moon, Dyad Moon.

This month we will see a super full moon, or supermoon, on the 14th. The moon's orbit is not a perfect circle, and through every month it is sometimes closer, sometimes further away. When the closest point happens to coincide with a full moon, we have a super full moon, which can be noticeably bigger and brighter than other full moons.

New moon

This month's new moon on the 29th is in Cancer. Astrologers believe that the new moon is a good time to make plans and focus on your dreams and hopes for the period ahead, and that each new moon has a particular energy, depending on which zodiacal sign it is in. Cancer is the sign governing home and family, making this a good time to plan and begin projects designed to increase your domestic bliss.

The first sighting of the new crescent moon on or around the 30th signals the beginning of Dhul-Hijjah, the Islamic month of pilgrimage, and the Hajj, one of the world's major pilgrimages.

Moon phases for June

1st	2nd	3rd	4th	5th
6th	7th	8th	9th	10th
11th	12th	13th	14th FULL	15th
16th	17th	18th	19th	20th
21st	22nd	23rd	24th	25th
26th	27th	28th	29th NEW	30th

J

THE GARDEN

Gardening by the moon

Summer is really here, the long days followed by warm nights.
This month sees a final push to get plants into the ground
or their final pots, before the work switches to maintenance:
watering, feeding, weeding and – eventually – cropping. Despite
this being midsummer, the warmest months are still ahead of
us due to the thermal lag in the seas and earth, which release
their warmth slowly like a storage heater. The frenzied work
of spring is behind us, and there is time to just sit in those long,
warm dusks, and enjoy the garden.

Whether you are gardening in time with the moon or not,
use the following as a guide to jobs to do in June.

Note: Sometimes these dates differ from those in the
moon phase chart on page 127, to take into account sensible
gardening hours. Where no specific time for the change
between phases is mentioned, this is because it happens
early in the morning or late at night. For exact changeover
times for any late-night or pre-dawn gardening, refer to the
moon phase chart.

New moon to 1st quarter: 30th May (from 12.30)–7th (till 15.48) and 29th–6th July

Rising vitality and upward growth. Plant and sow anything
that develops above ground towards the end of phase. Prepare
for growth.

- You can sow or plant out everything mentioned in the next
  moon phase, particularly towards the end of this phase.
- Pot on chillies and tomatoes into their final pots.
- Plant out bedding and hanging baskets. Water baskets
  every day.

1st quarter to full moon: 7th (from 15.48)–14th (till 12.51)

Sow crops that develop above ground, don't sow root crops.
Plant out seedlings and young plants. Take cuttings and make
grafts. Avoid other pruning. Fertilise.

- Plant out any remaining spring-sown plants.

- Plant out bedding and hanging baskets. Water baskets every day. Feed weekly.
- Place brassica collars around the stems of brassicas to keep cabbage root fly out. Net against cabbage white butterflies.
- Plant sweetcorn in a block, with plants 35cm apart.
- Plant tomatoes into the ground or final pots in the greenhouse, with sturdy support. Nip out side shoots on cordon varieties. Feed weekly with high potash fertiliser.
- Sow beetroot, carrots, courgettes, cucumbers, French and runner beans, kale, peas, swedes and turnips in small amounts direct or into pots to plant out when space opens up.
- Sow small amounts of coriander, chervil, dill, parsley and basil indoors in pots, or direct.

Full moon to 3rd quarter: 14th (from 12.51)–20th
A 'drawing down' energy. Sow and plant crops that develop below ground: root crops, bulbs and perennials.
- Sow 'maincrop' varieties of carrots. Sow autumn beetroot, swedes, turnips and spring onions.
- Pot up strawberry runners.
- Lift, divide and replant overcrowded clumps of spring bulbs.

3rd quarter to new moon: 21st–28th
A dormant period, with low sap and poor growth. Do not sow or plant. Prune, weed and harvest crops for storage. Fertilise and mulch. Garden maintenance.
- The asparagus season ends at the summer solstice, 21st June. Stop cropping and allow the plants to grow ferny. Feed regularly with a balanced fertiliser.
- Net strawberries.
- Earth up potatoes.
- Weed.
- Tie growing crops into supports.
- Inspect lilies for scarlet lily beetle and their larvae.
- Deadhead roses as they fade.

NATURE

Birds of the month – dove and pigeon

The dove is a symbol of Pentecost, which falls on 5th June this year. Doves are generally smaller than pigeons but they are in the same family of birds (Columbidae), which consists of over 300 species. There are several dove relatives that we can see in our gardens and towns.

The feral pigeon is most probably the bird that many of us see most often, as it has become extremely – often annoyingly – adapted to living on the scraps and mess that humans leave behind. Feral pigeons are descended from escaped domestic pigeons, bred for eating, which in turn are descended from rock doves. Rock doves inhabit sea cliffs and mountain ledges on the northern and western coasts of Scotland, on offshore islands and on the coast of Northern Ireland. Feral pigeons settle wherever they can find crannies that resemble cliff ledges, often the struts under bridges and the nooks of office blocks. They are grey, stout and sturdy but their grey necks are overlaid with iridescent pink and green, like an oil slick on a tarmac road.

Collared doves are more delicate: slim, pale and distinguished. They have a thin black collar at their neck, and their grey breast has a blush of pink to it. They can often make truly shocking nests, really just a few twigs piled loosely on top of each other with the eggs perched precariously on top. Collared doves are responsible for the soft but relentless 'coo-COOOO-coo' noise that echoes around your house when they perch on top of your chimney.

The turtle dove is an even daintier thing, and sadly far more endangered. It is a bird of Britain's east coast, but increasingly rare there. You might notice it by its gentle, telephone-like purring coo. It is small, only a little larger than a blackbird, and has a pink-blushed grey breast, black gill-like markings on its neck, and brown and black patterned wings.

TURTLE DOVE

COLLARED DOVE

FERAL PIGEON

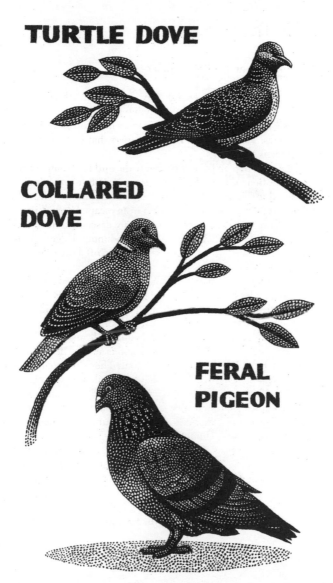

J

THE KITCHEN

What a month of gorgeous bounty in the kitchen, and all of it delicate and delicious. Although we have become used to strawberries of a kind being available all year round, this is their month, when they will be perfumed, flavourful and dripping with juice. Visit a fruit farm and then head to the kitchen with your mounded baskets to capture fragrant summer in numerous jars: the preparation for dark days must always begin during the brightest ones.

The kitchen garden is finally giving more than it takes, and this month should see an abundance of young, fresh produce: peas, broad beans and baby courgettes, lettuces and globe artichokes.

In the sea, mackerel is at its most abundant, and crab and lobster are in season. Young, fresh cheeses are arriving as the dairy farms make the most of the good new milk. This is a month in which it is easy to eat well.

In season

In the hedgerows, woods and fields
Wild greens: Cleavers, hairy bittercress, hedge garlic, lemon balm, wild marjoram, pineapple weed, spearmint, sweet cicely, watercress, water mint, wild thyme, wild fennel
Edible wild flowers: Broom, borage, elderflowers, chamomile, hawthorn, honeysuckle, lime, marigolds, meadowsweet, nasturtiums, pansies, red clover, wild roses
Wild fruits: Wild strawberries, wild gooseberries

From the seashore and rivers
Fish and shellfish: Mackerel, sea trout, brown crab, herring, lobster, turbot, sardines, salmon
Seaweeds: Laver, pepper dulse, carragheen, egg wrack, sea lettuce, sugar kelp

From the kitchen garden
Fruits: Gooseberries, strawberries, blackcurrants, cherries, loganberries, raspberries, redcurrants, rhubarb
Vegetables: Globe artichokes, asparagus, calabrese, carrots, courgettes, cucumbers, broad beans, cauliflowers, chard, endive, lettuces, spring greens, spring onions, new potatoes, radishes, wild rocket, spinach, beetroot, garlic, peas, turnips
Herbs: Chives, basil, mint, dill, marjoram, thyme, oregano

From the farms
Asparagus, Cheddar Valley strawberries, Ayrshire and Cornish new potatoes, goat's cheese, Stinking Bishop, ewe's curd, ricotta, new season lamb

And traditional imports
Alphonso mango, apricots, peaches, nectarines, cherries

J

RECIPES

Biscuit of the month

Goosnargh cakes

Very much not cakes, these caraway-scented biscuits originated in the village of Goosnargh in Lancashire and were traditionally baked and eaten with ale at Whitsuntide. Whitsun falls on 5th June this year.

Makes 15–20
Ingredients
110g butter, softened
75g caster sugar
175g plain flour
1 ½ teaspoon caraway seeds
Pinch of salt

Method

Link a baking sheet with nonstick baking paper. Cream the butter and 50g of the sugar until light and fluffy. Mix in the flour, caraway seeds and salt, then use your hands to bring the mixture together into a dough. Knead briefly and roll out on a lightly floured surface to 5mm thickness. Cut into 5cm rounds and arrange on the lined baking sheet. Chill in the fridge for 30 minutes.

Preheat the oven to 180°C, Gas Mark 4. Sprinkle the remaining sugar over the tops, and then bake for 15 minutes. Cool completely before eating.

Green *fattoush* with yoghurt and hot chilli oil

Fattoush is a Middle Eastern salad made hearty by the
addition of torn chunks of pitta, which soak up the juices.
It is normally made with tomatoes and cucumbers but as we
are a little early for those, this version makes use of all of the
beautiful green vegetables now coming through in the garden.

Serves 6
Ingredients
¼ red onion, finely sliced
Juice of ¾ lemon
75g green beans, topped and tailed and cut into 5cm lengths
75g fresh or frozen peas
100g broad beans
50g mangetout or sugar snap peas, topped and tailed and chopped in half
1 small head of lettuce, torn into pieces
Large handful of basil leaves, torn
3 pitta breads
80ml extra virgin olive oil
Salt and pepper

Mint yoghurt with hot chilli oil
40ml extra virgin olive oil
Pinch of chilli powder
¼ teaspoon smoked paprika
Juice of ¼ lemon
6 tablespoons full fat yoghurt
Leaves from a sprig of mint, finely chopped
Salt and pepper

Method

Put the onion slices into a bowl, then pour boiling water over them and set aside for 20 minutes. Drain and return it to a bowl and mix in a little of the lemon juice while you assemble the rest of the salad ingredients. Steam the green beans, peas and broad beans for just 2 minutes (yes, even the frozen ones), so that they are still crunchy. Blanch them in very cold water and then drain. Slip the broad beans out of their skins – this takes a little while but is so worth it. Lay all on some kitchen paper to dry off and then tip into a large salad bowl with the mangetout or sugar snap peas, lettuce and basil leaves.

Toast the pittas then tear into bite-sized chunks and add them, too. Tip in the olive oil and the rest of the lemon juice, and stir to coat everything. Season with salt and pepper.

For the chilli oil, put 25ml of the olive oil in a small pan and add the chilli powder, smoked paprika and lemon juice. Heat until it bubbles, then remove from the heat.

For the mint yoghurt, mix the yoghurt with the mint, the remaining olive oil, a pinch of salt and a grind or two of pepper. Transfer to a small bowl, swirling the surface to make ridges and furrows. When the chilli oil has cooled a little, pour it onto the surface of the mint yoghurt and swirl it in a little. Serve alongside the salad.

FOLK STORY OF THE MONTH

Merlin and the Making of Stonehenge

For hundreds of years – even as late as the 18th century – the folk belief about the construction of Stonehenge was based on that put forward by Geoffrey of Monmouth (c.1100–c.1155) in his chronicle *The History of the Kings of Britain* (c.1136). This is how the story goes.

To commemorate the hundreds of Britons treacherously slaughtered on Salisbury Plain during a supposed truce with the Saxons, King Aurelius Conanus decided to build a great monument. He set his carpenters and stonemasons to the task but they failed to come up with a plan grand or impressive enough, and so he sent for Merlin. Merlin said, 'If you want to grace the burial place of these men with a suitable monument, send for the Giant's Ring which is on Mount Killaraus in Ireland. There you will find a stone construction that no man of this age could erect unless he combined great skill and artistry. The stones are enormous and no man alive could move them. If they are placed in the same way around this site, then they will stand for ever.' The stones at Mount Killaraus had been placed there by two giants who had stolen them from Africa for their healing qualities, and would pour water over them and then use it to fill baths and heal the sick.

Merlin, together with the king's brother, Uther Pendragon, and 15,000 men, readied ships and set off for Ireland. There they battled and vanquished Irish forces and set about the stones. But the stones, being so vast, proved impossible to move, so Merlin used his magic to move them to the ships. Once they had been transported to Salisbury Plain, Aurelius ordered Merlin to erect the stones in the same pattern in which they had been arranged in Ireland, and he did so, and Stonehenge was created. After their deaths, Uther Pendragon and Aurelius were buried within the ring of stones.

FOLK SONG OF THE MONTH

'Midsummer Carol (Lemady)'
Traditional, arr. Richard Barnard

This traditional West Country ballad makes reference to
Midsummer wooing. On Midsummer's morning young men
would get up at dawn to gather posies of flowers and present
them to the object of their affections, a practice known as
'lemady'.

A midsummer morning as I was a-walking
The fields and the meadows were green and gay,
The birds sang so sweetly, so sweet and adoring
So early in the morning at break of day.
The birds sang so sweetly etc.

It's hark, O hark to the nightingale singing,
The lark she is taking her flight in the air,
The turtle doves now in the green bough are building,
The sun is just a-glimm'ring, arise my fair.
The turtle doves now etc.

Arise and arise, go and gather a posy,
The sweetest of flowers that grow in yonder grove.
O, I'll pick them all, lilies, pinks and roses;
It's all for my Lemady, the girl I love.
O, I'll pick them all etc.

O, Lemady! O, Lemady! The sweetest of flowers,
The sweetest of flowers my eyes did ever see
And I'll play a tune on the pipes of ivory
So early in the morning at break of day.
And I'll play a tune etc.

July

7 7th–12th: Hajj – Muslim pilgrimage to Mecca

9 Wimbledon Women's Final

10 Wimbledon Men's Final

10 Sea Sunday (Christian)

12 Battle of the Boyne – bank holiday, Northern Ireland

15 St Swithin's Day (Christian/traditional)

23 Birthday of Haile Selassie (Rastafarian)

29 Al Hijra – Islamic New Year, start of the Islamic year 1444, begins at the sighting of the new moon (Muslim)

DRESSING UP IN JULY

Rose Queens

A number of villages around the UK will see the crowning of their Rose Queen this month. Rose Queen coronations arose mainly in areas where there was a stronger tradition of 'Wakes Week' than of May Day celebrations. Wakes Week was the name adopted by factory owners for the weeks (and later fortnights) when they would shut their factories down and give the whole workforce their holiday at once, as a more economical alternative to staggered holidays. Local festivals and fêtes in the newly industrialised towns of the Midlands and the North of England, especially the Northwest, often took on the name 'wakes'. The organisers of these wakes may have simply fancied a May Queen-like tradition, but the wakes fell in the summer rather than the spring and so Rose Queens were created. They are essentially May Queens – teenage girls or young women dressed in white and garlanded with flowers – but with roses rather than lily of the valley and bluebells in their hair.

Several of these traditions appear to have been started, or revived, by the would-be Rose Queens themselves. For example, the first Rose Queen coronation in the village of Wrea Green in Lancashire occurred in July 1924 when a group of seven local girls who had watched a Rose Queen procession in a nearby village decided that they should have one of their own. They chose a queen and attendants and made a rose crown, then set off around the village green, but only got part way round before losing their nerve and retreating to a local garden for the coronation. Since then there have been over 70 Rose Queens in the village, and the coronation has become a central part of Wrea Green's Field Day festivities.

Although Rose Queen festivals are much less common now than they were a century ago, they can still be found at villages around the country. Sutton in St Helens, Merseyside, and Langho, in Lancashire, recently celebrated the 25th and 50th anniversaries respectively of their Rose Queen festivals.

THE SKY

A quiet month in the evening sky, but Jupiter is rising earlier now and you may catch a glimpse of it if you are out stargazing late. It will continue to rise earlier each night. The term 'dog days' is applied to the spell of hot, humid weather we sometimes experience at the end of July. This comes from ancient Egypt and refers to the fact that the dog star, Sirius, the brightest star in the sky, now rises in the pre-dawn sky just before the sun, when seen from Cairo. We won't see the dog star in the UK and Ireland for another month, though.

At night

9th: Jupiter and the waning moon will rise together at around midnight in the east. They will be visible until lost in the dawn at 04.30 at an altitude of 38 degrees.

By day

4th: Aphelion. This is the moment in the year when the earth is furthest from the sun, in its elliptical orbit. At 08.10 the sun will be 152,098,455km away (compare with perihelion on 4th January, see page 13).

21st: At solar noon (approximately 13.00 BST/IST) the sun will reach an altitude of 59 degrees in the London sky and 50 degrees in the Glasgow sky.

1st–31st: Day length decreases this month by 1h 15m at Clitheroe, Lancashire.

J

Sunrise and set
Clitheroe, Lancashire

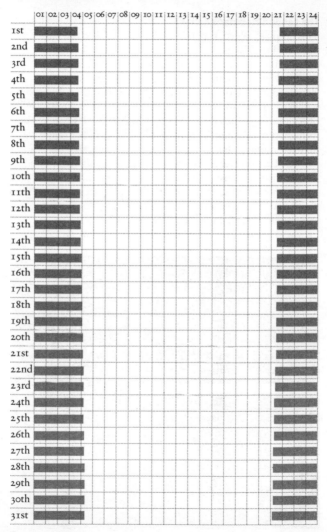

Deep-sky objects

The Lagoon Nebula/Messier 8

This deep-sky object is barely visible to the naked eye but is included here as it is easily found, and with a dark sky and the magnification of a pair of binoculars or a telescope it is beautiful and fascinating. The Lagoon Nebula is a large gas cloud about three times the size of the full moon. To find it you will need to look for the 'teapot' asterism in the constellation of Sagittarius, which never rises very high into the sky but is at its highest in the summer months. Look to its upper right. You may see a smudge but, if not, zoom in with your magnification.

The Lagoon Nebula is a giant, interstellar, star-forming cloud of gas and dust, which appears pink in time-exposure colour photographs, though it will look white to your eye. Only about two million years old, it is full of young, hot stars and star clusters, which are responsible for its glow. It is 110 by 50 light years across and 4,100 light years away from earth.

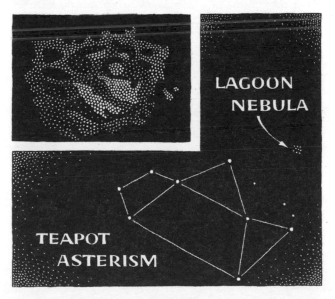

J

THE SEA

Average sea temperature

Shetland:	12.7°C
Greenock:	13.6°C
Cleethorpes:	14.7°C
Rhyl:	15.6°C
Rosslare:	14.7°C
Bideford:	16.2°C
Deal:	16.1°C

Spring and neap tides

Spring tides are the most extreme tides of the month, with the highest rises and the lowest falls, and they follow a couple of days after the full moon and new moon. Neap tides are the least extreme, with the smallest movement, and they fall in between the spring tides.

Spring tides: 1st–3rd, 14th–16th and 29th–31st

Neap tides: 8th–9th and 22nd–24th

Spring tides are shaded in black in the chart opposite.

July tide timetable for Dover

For guidance on how to convert this for your local area, see page 8.

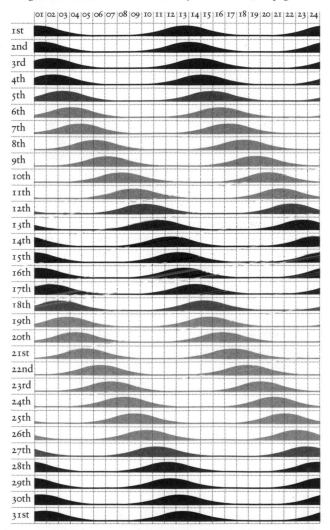

THE MOON

Moon phases

1st quarter – 7th July, 03.14

Full moon – 13th July, 19.37

3rd quarter – 20th July, 15.18

New moon – 28th July, 18.54

Full moon

Names for July's full moon: Wyrt Moon, Mead Moon.

This will be another super full moon (see page 121).

New moon

July's new moon this year is in Leo. Astrologers believe that the new moon is a good time to make plans and focus on your dreams and hopes for the period ahead, and that each new moon has a particular energy, depending on which zodiacal sign it is in. Leo is a confident and energetic sign, so the new moon on the 28th would be a good moment to plan or begin projects involving fun and self-promotion.

Moon phases for July

1st	2nd	3rd	4th	5th
6th	7th	8th	9th	10th
11th	12th	13th FULL	14th	15th
16th	17th	18th	19th	20th
21st	22nd	23rd	24th	25th
26th	27th	28th NEW	29th	30th
31st				

J

THE GARDEN

Gardening by the moon

July can be one of our warmest months, but it can also be one of the stormiest times of the year, plus there is St Swithin's Day on the 15th to contend with: the weather on that day, rain or shine, is said to set in for 40 days. Although this rarely happens, weather patterns in mid-July do often set a trend that continues into August, so fingers crossed St Swithin comes through with some sunshine. Apple growers have always wished for rain on the day, however, as it is seen as St Swithin watering the orchards and christening the apples.

Whether you are gardening in time with the moon or not, use the following as a guide to jobs to do in July.

Note: Sometimes these dates differ from those in the moon phase chart on page 149, to take into account sensible gardening hours. Where no specific time for the change between phases is mentioned, this is because it happens early in the morning or late at night. For exact changeover times for any late-night or pre-dawn gardening, refer to the moon phase chart.

New moon to 1st quarter: 29th June–6th and 29th–5th August (till 12.06)

Rising vitality and upward growth. Plant and sow anything that develops above ground towards the end of phase. Prepare for growth.

- You can sow, plant out or take cuttings of all of those things mentioned in the next moon phase, but towards the end of this phase is better.

1st quarter to full moon: 7th–13th

Sow crops that develop above ground, don't sow root crops. Plant out seedlings and young plants. Take cuttings and make grafts. Avoid other pruning. Fertilise.

- Sow French beans and peas for autumn harvesting.
- Finish planting out winter brassicas. Earth up stems and protect with netting.

- Sow salad leaves for autumn and winter harvesting: mustard greens, mizuna, mibuna, pak choi and chop suey greens, as well as kale, rocket, lettuces and Swiss chard.
- Take cuttings of woody herbs such as rosemary, sage and thyme.
- Feed everything.

Full moon to 3rd quarter: 14th–20th (till 15.18)
A 'drawing down' energy. Sow and plant crops that develop below ground: root crops, bulbs and perennials.
- Last chance to sow beetroot for autumn harvesting.
- Continue to sow late maincrop carrot and turnip varieties, and spring onions.
- Plant out leeks.
- Pot up strawberry runners to make new plants to plant out next year.

3rd quarter to new moon: 20th (from 15.18)–28th
A dormant period, with low sap and poor growth. Do not sow or plant. Prune, weed and harvest crops for storage. Fertilise and mulch. Garden maintenance.
- Young fruit on apples and pears needs to be thinned to allow room for those left behind to develop.
- Pinch out the sideshoots on cordon tomatoes and continue to feed regularly with a high potash feed, tying stems in as they grow.
- Pinch out the tops of climbing beans when they reach the tops of their frames. Spray the flowers of runner beans with water in hot weather to encourage pollination.
- Harvest onions, garlic and shallots for storage now if you can. You need a dry spell of weather: lay them in the sun to dry out.
- Weed regularly.
- Earth up potatoes.
- Prune cherries and plums if they need pruning.
- Thin grapes and prune sideshoots.
- Cut the fruited canes of summer raspberries to the ground and tie in new growth.

THE KITCHEN

In July, the garden produce is plentiful and delicious: if ever
there was a time for a picnic, it is now.

In season

In the hedgerows, woods and fields
Wild herbs: Cleavers, hairy bittercress, hedge garlic, lemon
balm, wild marjoram, pineapple weed, spearmint, sweet cicely,
watercress, water mint, wild thyme, wild fennel
Edible wild flowers: Borage, chamomile, hawthorn,
honeysuckle, lime, marigolds, meadowsweet, nasturtiums
(flowers and seeds), pansies, red clover, wild roses
Wild fruits and nuts: Wild strawberries, cherry plums, wild
gooseberries, green walnuts for pickling
Game: Wood pigeon

From the seashore and rivers
Fish and shellfish: Mackerel, brown crab, herring, lobster,
turbot, sea trout, black bream, sea bass, sardines, salmon
Samphire

From the kitchen garden
Fruits: Blackcurrants, gooseberries, loganberries, raspberries,
cherries, blueberries
Vegetables: French beans, runner beans, broad beans,
courgettes (and their flowers), cucumbers, globe artichokes,
peas, fennel, shallots, rhubarb, beetroot, calabrese, cabbages,
carrots, cauliflowers, chard, endive, garlic, lettuces, spring
onions, new potatoes, radishes, wild rocket, turnips
Herbs and edible flowers: Mint, basil, dill, chives, marjoram,
thyme, oregano, calendula flowers

From the farms
Cherries, goat's cheeses, ewe's curd, ricotta, new season lamb

And traditional imports
Apricots, peaches, nectarines, cherries

RECIPES

Biscuit of the month

Pressed-flower biscuits

Bake edible flowers onto these lemon- and rosewater-scented biscuits and they will look like perfect botanical specimens.

Makes about 20
Ingredients
100g butter, softened
50g golden caster sugar
Seeds of 1 vanilla pod
½ teaspoon rosewater
1 large egg yolk
150g plain flour
25g cornflour
Selection of edible flowers – such as rose, marigold and cornflower petals, scented geranium, pea and viola flowers – sandwiched between sheets of kitchen paper and pressed for a few hours between heavy books
4 teaspoons icing sugar, sieved
Approximately 1 teaspoon lemon juice

Method

Preheat the oven to 180°C, Gas Mark 4 and line a baking sheet with nonstick baking paper. Cream the butter, sugar, vanilla seeds and rosewater and then beat in the egg yolk. Sift in the flour and cornflour, and mix together to form a dough. Roll out on a lightly floured surface to a thickness of 3mm and cut into 5cm rounds. Place on the lined baking sheet and lay the petals or whole flowers onto the surface of the biscuits, pressing them in slightly. Bake for 12–14 minutes or until the biscuits are just starting to turn golden. Remove and cool on a wire rack. Mix the icing sugar with enough lemon juice to make a thin glaze, and paint it over each of the biscuits. Leave to dry before eating.

Griddled peach, halloumi and serrano ham salad

A collection of delicious summery things that happen to sit alongside each other very well, this is a good use for any peaches or nectarines that are less than perfectly ripe. Grill on the barbecue on a sunny day or on a griddle on the hob when you want to pretend it's sunny.

Serves 2 as a main meal or 4 as a side dish

Ingredients

Large handful of watercress

Leaves from a small bunch of basil, torn

Leaves from a sprig of mint, chopped finely

2 peaches or nectarines, stoned and cut into eighths

6 tablespoons extra virgin olive oil

1 packet of halloumi, sliced thickly

Juice of 1 lemon

6 pieces of serrano ham

Salt and pepper

Method

Put the watercress into a salad bowl. Add the torn basil leaves and chopped mint leaves. Put the peach or nectarine slices into a second bowl with the olive oil, and turn them until they are coated, then lay each piece on the barbecue or griddle, reserving the oil. Turn after a minute or so, once the griddle lines have appeared. Place the halloumi slices on the barbecue or griddle and do the same. Mix the reserved olive oil and lemon juice and season with salt and pepper. Add two-thirds of it to the bowl of leaves, and turn the leaves until they are coated. Divide the leaves between plates and arrange the peaches or nectarines, halloumi and serrano ham on top of them. Drizzle with the last of the dressing, and eat immediately.

Tortilla de patatas – Spanish omelette

The most famous miracle performed by St Swithin – whose feast day falls on the 15th July – was mending broken eggs. Workmen building the bridge he had ordered in Winchester jostled an elderly egg-seller, causing all of her eggs to fall to the ground and crack. St Swithin picked up the eggs and made them whole again. But he could have made this.

Serves 4
Ingredients
2 large potatoes (about 700g), peeled
80ml extra virgin olive oil
6 large eggs
Salt and pepper

Method

Cut the potatoes into quarters, then chop until you have 5mm-thick slices, around 2–3cm long and 2–3cm wide. Tip them onto a tea towel and pat dry.

Pour the oil into a nonstick frying pan over a medium heat and warm for a couple of minutes, then tip in all of the potatoes. Stir to coat them in oil. Season with salt and pepper and keep on cooking, stirring often, for about 25 minutes or until the potatoes are cooked through.

Crack the eggs into a large bowl, season with salt and pepper, and beat. Tip the potatoes into the egg mixture and stir to mix well. Reduce the heat to low and tip the potato and egg mixture into the pan. Cook for 4 minutes, occasionally running a spatula around the edge and shaking the pan to make sure the tortilla isn't sticking. Place a large plate over the top, invert the pan and plate, and then slide the tortilla into the pan, uncooked side down. Use your spatula to push the edges in to tidy the tortilla up. Cook for a further 4 minutes and then slide the cooked tortilla onto a plate.

NATURE

Bird of the month – the tit

The name 'tit' for this group of small songbirds comes from 'titmouse', which in turn is from the Middle English word *titmose*, in which *tit* refers to any small creature and *mose* means 'bird'. It seems likely that *mose* turned into 'mouse' because of these birds' quick, darting, mouse-like movements. Hugely active, lively and acrobatic, they are always on the move. Tits were originally woodland birds, but some species have adapted well to life in our gardens and can often be seen on bird tables and hanging off of fat balls.

Blue tits are the most common tits in our gardens, easily identified by their blue wings and caps – which can be raised into a little crest – their green backs and yellow breasts. They make a lot of noise: a high-pitched whistling 'tsee-tsee' and then a descending trill, plus an angry, churring alarm call. They produce just one brood per year.

Great tits are larger and bolder, often bordering on violence at the bird table. A great tit has a yellow breast with a black band down it, and the black also runs up and covers its head, apart from its white cheeks. Most often its call is a confident descending pair of notes, repeated, often described as 'tea-cher, tea-cher', but it will make ascending runs of two or three notes, too.

Coal tits are more often found in woodlands. The coal tit is the smallest of the tits, with a dumpy body and a short tail. It has strident black and white head markings, a grey back and wings, and a buff-coloured underside. It also makes the 'tea-cher, tea-cher' call, but higher and faster than the great tit.

GREAT TIT

COAL TIT

BLUE TIT

J

FOLK STORY OF THE MONTH

The Weardale Fairies

A key element in this story of fairy folk is the glow-worm, a beetle famous for the greenish-orange light that the females emit at night – but only in June–July.

A young farmer's daughter who lived in Stanhope, on Weardale in the Pennines, was out gathering wild flowers when she heard beautiful music, played on the pipe, fiddle and drum. Beguiled, she followed the sound to a cleft between two rocks, and looking through the crack she could see fairy folk dancing by candlelight. She knew it wasn't safe to linger, so she tore herself away to run home.

Her parents were horrified when she told them. 'Oh, my love, we have as good as lost you!' cried the mother. 'The fairy folk hate to be spied upon and they will come and fetch you tonight.' They put every possible protection in place, but in the morning the girl was gone. The distraught father set off for the local wise woman's house and begged her to tell him how to win his daughter back. 'You must take the fairies three gifts,' said the woman. 'A light that does not burn; a part of an animal gained without shedding blood; and a live chicken without a bone in its body.' The farmer thanked her, but set off full of despair.

Along the road he was roused from his troubles by a scrawny beggar, and he dropped the poor man a coin. The beggar said, 'I have little to give you in return, but take this glow-worm I use to light my way at night.' The farmer was astonished and accepted the glow-worm with great thanks. Walking further, he noticed a lizard struggling in a twist of wire and so he bent down to free it, but as he did so the lizard's tail came away in his hand and the lizard scuttled away, unharmed. Feeling happier by the moment, the farmer continued along the road. Soon he heard a great struggle in the bushes and saw a thrush being attacked by a hawk. He threw a stone and hit the hawk, and as the thrush flew away, it sang, 'An egg under a hen! An egg under a hen!' The farmer rushed home and, taking a warm egg from under his broody hen, he set off for the fairy's lair. When he heard the music, he looked through the cleft in the rocks and spied his daughter, pale and exhausted, dancing with the fairy folk.

'I bring you three gifts in exchange for my daughter!' he shouted, and he pushed the gifts through the gap. In a moment there was a great crash and a flash of light, then all fell silent and dark in the rock. The farmer's heart sank, but then from behind him came a voice crying, 'Father!' – and there was his daughter, laughing and smiling and ready to return safely home…and to never, ever spy on the fairy folk again.

FOLK SONG OF THE MONTH

'The Rose and the Lily (The Cruel Brother)'
Traditional, arr. Richard Barnard

In this tragic ballad the woman's crime seems to be simply
that she failed to seek her brother's permission before
marrying. The two summer flowers here represent the two
siblings, one (the rose) symbolic of beauty and femininity,
the other (the lily) of death. (The structure of the first two
verses should be followed for the remaining verses.)

There were three maids a-playing ball
With a high lily-O,
There were three maids a-playing ball
And came three Lords to court them all.
For the rose is sweet, I know.

The first who came was all in white
With a high lily-O,
The first who came was all in white
And asked one maid to be his wife.
For the rose is sweet, I know.

The next who came was all in green
And took one maid to be his queen.

The next who came was all in red
And asked the last if she would wed.

'Then you must ask my father dear,
Likewise of her that did me bear,

And you must ask my brother John,
And also of my sister Anne.'

'Well, I have asked your father dear,
Likewise of her that did you bear,

And I have asked your sister Anne,
But I've not asked your brother John.'

For on the road they rode along
Then did they meet her brother John.

She stooped down low to kiss him sweet,
He to her heart did a dagger meet.

'I wish I were on yonder stile,
There I would sit and bleed awhile

I wish I were on yonder hill,
There I'd alight and make my will.'

'What would you give your sister Anne?'
'My gay gold ring and feathered fan.'

'What would you give your father dear?'
'The gallant steed which doth me bear.'

'What would you give your mother dear?'
'My wedding dress that I wore here,

But she must wash it very clean
So my heart's blood can ne'er be seen.'

'What would you give your brother John?'
'A rope and gallows to hang him on.'

August

1 Lammas (Christian) and Lughnasadh (Gaelic/pagan/neopagan)

1 Summer bank holiday, Scotland

1 August bank holiday, Ireland

6 6th–7th: Tisha B'Av – Jewish day of mourning, begins at sundown

15 The Assumption of Mary (Christian)

18 Krishna Janmashtami – Krishna's birthday (Hindu)

25 Calypso Monarch Finals – climax of UK calypso season

27 27–29 Notting Hill Carnival, London

29 Summer bank holiday, England, Wales, Northern Ireland

30 Ganesh Chaturthi – birth of Ganesh (Hindu)

DRESSING UP IN AUGUST

Moko Jumbies at Notting Hill Carnival

At the end of August, Moko Jumbies will stalk the streets of west London during the Notting Hill Carnival. These stilt-walkers are up to 4.5m tall, with painted faces and colourful costumes. They are a link back through the origins of Carnival in Trinidad to the folklore of the west coast of Africa, from where so many people were taken into slavery and transported to the Caribbean islands.

The Trinidadian Carnival began as a pre-Lent, Mardi Gras masquerade among French and Spanish settlers. Slave masters would black up and dress as field slaves, or *nègres de jardin*, and their wives would dress as the *mulatresses*, the women of mixed racial origin who were the children of raped slaves. On the abolition of slavery in 1834 the Carnival became popular among the emancipated former slaves, and the tradition was turned on its head: comedy characters such as Dame Lorraine – a white woman with huge bosom and bottom – became regulars, and revellers wore white masks and stuffed clothes that mocked the plantation owners. Moko Jumbies became standard characters at around the same time: Moko is a West African god of retribution, and the word Jumbie, which was added later, means 'spirit'. Moko Jumbies are protective spirits, able to see trouble coming from their great height. In Trinidad they were thought to reside in the big old silk cotton trees on plantations where so many slaves were hanged.

The 'Windrush generation', West Indians who answered the call to emigrate to the UK to help reduce Britain's post-war labour shortages, found themselves in an often hostile land. In January 1959, the journalist Claudia Jones introduced Carnival arts and culture to London when she held an indoor carnival event to unite the community after the Notting Hill riots of August 1958. Then, in the summer of 1966, Rhaune Laslett started the Notting Hill Festival with children dressed in costume, joined by musicians. This was the birth of the carnival street parade, which now attracts over a million revellers. Some of the traditional costumes have died out, but the Moko Jumbies can still be seen, high above, watching over the festival-goers.

THE SKY

As well as the prolific Perseids meteor shower, we have Saturn at opposition this month. This means that it is in the opposite part of our sky from the sun, creating a 'full Saturn' in the same way that we see a full moon when the moon and sun are either side of us. It will be well placed for evening viewing, and its rings will be presented at a good angle so that if you have a small telescope or even a good pair of binoculars you should be able to see them. Look out also for the first appearance of Sirius, the dog star, the brightest star in the sky, which will appear in the dawn around the third week of August.

At night

12th–13th: Perseids meteor shower. The best time for viewing will be from 22.00 on the 12th until 04.00 on the 13th. The radiant will be at about 40 degrees altitude in the northeast at midnight. Unfortunately, the full moon will obscure all but the brightest trails.

13th–14th: Saturn at opposition. It will first appear in the dusk at around 21.00, low in the southeast sky. It reaches a maximum altitude of 22 degrees at midnight in the south, and gets lost in the dawn at 05.30 in the southwest.

14th–15th: Conjunction of Jupiter and the waning moon. They will rise together at around 22.00 in the east and be visible until lost in the dawn at 05.30 while at an altitude of 34 degrees.

By day

21st: At solar noon (approximately 13.00 BST/IST) the sun will reach an altitude of 50 degrees in the London sky and 46 degrees in the Glasgow sky.

1st–31st: Day length decreases this month by 2h 1m in Clitheroe, Lancashire.

A

Sunrise and set
Clitheroe, Lancashire

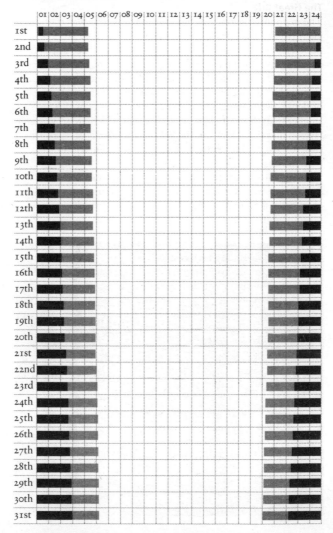

Deep-sky objects

The Great Rift

The main impression when looking at the Milky Way is of a
great river of stars processing through the heavens. But it is
not all stars – here and there are dark patches. These are dark
nebulae, also known as absorption nebulae. The largest of them
is the Great Rift, which cuts a path along the line of Cygnus, the
Swan. The absence of stars here is actually caused by a series
of dense, overlapping dust clouds, the particles of which are
smaller than those of cigarette smoke, but which are so vast and
layered that they block out the light of thousands of stars. Any
that you see 'within' those dark spaces are simply closer to us
than the dust clouds are.

Moonless nights from midsummer to September offer the
best chance to view the Great Rift. Through August it will be
at its highest point at around midnight. It will continue to be
prominent into September.

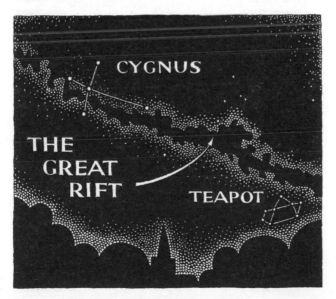

THE SEA

Average sea temperature

Shetland:	13.1°C
Greenock:	14.2°C
Cleethorpes:	15.6°C
Rhyl:	16.4°C
Rosslare:	15.4°C
Bideford:	17.1°C
Deal:	17.7°C

Spring and neap tides

Spring tides are the most extreme tides of the month, with the highest rises and the lowest falls, and they follow a couple of days after the full moon and new moon. Neap tides are the least extreme, with the smallest movement, and they fall in between the spring tides.

Spring tides: 13th–15th and 29th–31st

Neap tides: 6th–8th and 21st–22nd

Spring tides are shaded in black in the chart opposite.

August tide timetable for Dover

For guidance on how to convert this for your local area, see page 8.

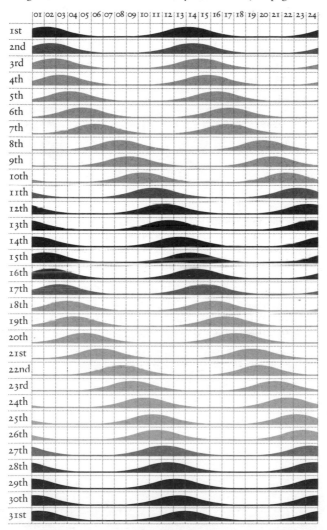

A

THE MOON

Moon phases

1st quarter – 5th August, 12.06

Full moon – 12th August, 02.35

3rd quarter – 19th August, 05.36

New moon – 27th August, 09.17

Full moon
Names for August's full moon: Grain Moon, Lynx Moon.

New moon
The new moon on the 27th is in Virgo. Astrologers believe that the new moon is a good time to make plans and focus on your dreams and hopes for the period ahead, and that each new moon has a particular energy, depending on which zodiacal sign it is in. Virgo is routine-focused, so this new moon would be a good time for fresh starts around organisation and health.

Moon phases for August

1st	2nd	3rd	4th	5th

6th	7th	8th	9th	10th

11th	12th FULL	13th	14th	15th

16th	17th	18th	19th	20th

21st	22nd	23rd	24th	25th

26th	27th NEW	28th	29th	30th

31st				

A

THE GARDEN

Gardening by the moon

It's as though a switch has been thrown in the garden in August: something has changed. The three months of burgeoning, galloping growth end and a mellow, lazy atmosphere has set in. It is perhaps lucky that the main task now is reaping what you have sown. This is the start of the harvest season, and Lammas on the 1st marks the start of the grain harvest, and of the first fruits. Right on cue, blackberries start turning inky purple, and shades of gold start creeping into the edges of the garden's greenery.

And this is a month when any vegetable gardener's trug floweth over. Harvest little and often as soon as things are ripe, only waiting for the correct moon period for produce that is to be stored.

Whether you are gardening in time with the moon or not, use the following as a guide to jobs to do in August.

Note: Sometimes these dates differ from those in the moon phase chart on page 171, to take into account sensible gardening hours. Where no specific time for the change between phases is mentioned, this is because it happens early in the morning or late at night. For exact changeover times for any late-night or pre-dawn gardening, refer to the moon phase chart.

New moon to 1st quarter: 29th July–5th (till 12.06) and 27th–3rd September
Rising vitality and upward growth. Plant and sow anything that develops above ground towards the end of phase. Prepare for growth.

- You can sow, plant out or take cuttings of all of those things mentioned in the next moon phase, but towards the end of this phase is better.

1st quarter to full moon: 5th (from 12.06)–11th
Sow crops that develop above ground, don't sow root crops.

Plant out seedlings and young plants. Take cuttings and make grafts. Avoid other pruning. Fertilise.

- Sow hardy annual flowers where you want them to bloom next year.
- Sow salad leaves – mustard greens, mizuna, mibuna, pak choi and chop suey greens, as well as kale, rocket, lettuces and Swiss chard.
- Take cuttings of scented geraniums.
- Feed everything.

Full moon to 3rd quarter: 12th–18th

A 'drawing down' energy. Sow and plant crops that develop below ground: root crops, bulbs and perennials.

- Sow your last batch of carrots and turnips.
- Plant strawberry plants.
- Sow green manures – alfalfa, field beans, grazing rye or phacelia – to protect bare soil over winter.

3rd quarter to new moon: 19th–26th

A dormant period, with low sap and poor growth. Do not sow or plant. Prune, weed and harvest crops for storage. Fertilise and mulch. Garden maintenance.

- Deadhead dahlias to keep new flowers coming.
- Weed regularly.
- Pinch out the sideshoots on cordon tomatoes and continue to feed regularly with a high potash feed and to tie the stems in as they grow. Once a plant has produced four or five tresses of tomatoes (six or seven on some cherry types), 'stop' the plant by nipping out the tip, so encouraging ripening rather than growing.
- Pinch out the tops of climbing beans when they reach the tops of their frames and spray the flowers of runner beans with water in hot weather to encourage pollination.
- Earth up potatoes.
- Tie in the new growth of blackberries and boysenberries so that their stems are horizontal or even slope downwards towards the tip.

A

NATURE

Bird of the month – gull

Of the many gulls that you may see during a trip to the seaside, by far the most likely is the herring gull. It is so ubiquitous that for many of us its cries and calls provide the backdrop to our summer holidays – atmospheric from afar, a proper pain on your chalet roof at 06.00. The herring gull is large and confident and can be an aggressive scavenger: watch your pasty if you're eating on the beach. The adult bird has a white head and breast and a grey back and wings with black wing tips. It has a yellow beak and pink legs and feet. In winter it can develop dark streaks on its head.

The black-headed gull is a sociable, noisy bird and, though plentiful on the coasts, it is also the most common inland gull. You are as likely to see it on salt marshes, reservoirs and freshly ploughed farmland as you are at the coast. Despite its name, its head only turns dark in summer and even then it is chocolate brown rather than black. In winter it is almost white all over except for its black wing tips. Black-headed gulls gather in small flocks and will often roost and feed together in larger groups. This gull's call is said to sound a little like laughter.

Also in the gull family, the kittiwake is only really seen at the coast. However, at any cliff colony of seabirds, it is likely to be the most numerous species. Thousands of pairs of kittiwakes balance on their precarious nests made on tiny ledges high above the foaming sea, creating a riot of noise. Unlike many gulls, it does not scrounge on dumps or beaches and instead always feeds at sea. It has a rounded head, large black eyes and a small beak compared with other gulls, giving it a much gentler look. Its head and breast are pure white, its back grey and its wing tips black, and it has black legs.

BLACK-HEADED GULL

KITTIWAKE

HERRING GULL

THE KITCHEN

While blackberries are ripening in the hedgerows, cherries are reaching the end of their season: all the more reason to make the most of them. Tomatoes are starting to ripen and sweetcorn is abundant. This is a time for holidays and good eating – barbecues and long, lazy lunches. In London, the end of the month brings the great street food fest that is Carnival.

In season

In the hedgerows, woods and fields
Wild herbs: Cleavers, hairy bittercress, hedge garlic, lemon balm, marjoram, spearmint, sweet cicely, watercress, water mint, wild thyme, wild fennel
Edible wild flowers: Broom, borage, chamomile, honeysuckle, marigolds, meadowsweet, nasturtiums (flowers and seeds), red clover, wild roses
Wild fruits and nuts: Cherry plums, rosehips, wild strawberries and gooseberries, bilberries, blackberries, rowan berries, cobnuts
Game: Grouse, wood pigeon

From the seashore and rivers
Fish and shellfish: Black bream, brown crab, herring, lobster, mackerel, sea trout, turbot, plaice, sardines, megrim sole, squid, salmon
Samphire, sea buckthorn

From the kitchen garden
Fruits: Plums, apples, pears, blackcurrants, blueberries, loganberries, melons, raspberries, redcurrants, strawberries, cherries
Vegetables: Sweetcorn, tomatoes, aubergines, French beans, runner beans, calabrese, fennel, courgettes, leeks, radishes, globe artichokes, beetroot, cabbages, carrots, cauliflowers, chard, cucumbers, endive, garlic, lettuces, shallots, onions, spring onions, sweet peppers, chilli peppers, peas, potatoes, wild rocket, spinach, turnips
Herbs: Marjoram, thyme, dill, basil, mint, oregano

From the farms
Cobnuts, cherries

RECIPES

Biscuit of the month

Trinbagonian milk biscuits
These big, soft biscuits flirt with the boundary between cake and biscuit and are even known as 'biscuit cakes' in some parts. They are traditional to Trinidad and Tobago, and are included here to allow us a nod to the birthplace of Notting Hill Carnival, in biscuit form.

Makes 6
Ingredients
60g butter, melted
120ml evaporated milk
100g caster sugar, plus 2 tablespoons for coating
350g plain flour
½ teaspoon baking powder
½ teaspoon bicarbonate of soda
¼ teaspoon salt

Method
Preheat the oven to 180°C, Gas Mark 4 and line a baking sheet with nonstick baking paper. Put the melted butter, evaporated milk and 100g caster sugar into a large bowl, and mix. Sieve in the flour, baking powder, bicarbonate of soda and salt. Mix. Use your hands to bring the dough together. Knead it for a minute and then pat it out on a lightly floured surface. Roll out to a thickness of 1–2cm and cut 10cm rounds to be traditional, or smaller if not. Put the 2 tablespoons sugar on a plate and press each biscuit down into it, then turn them over so that the sugar is on the top, and place them on the baking sheet. Sprinkle any remaining sugar over the tops. Bake for 10–12 minutes. They should be pale in colour and soft and cakey in the middle.

A

Coconut and chilli corn

Sweetcorn is at its sweetest and best this month. This is a Caribbean method of cooking corn that infuses it with coconut, chilli and herb flavours.

Serves 6
Ingredients
6 corn cobs
400ml can coconut milk
1 Scotch bonnet pepper
2 spring onions, roughly chopped
Leaves from a small bunch coriander, chopped
Leaves from a small bunch parsley, chopped
1 clove garlic, roughly chopped
Bunch of thyme
1 teaspoon salt

Method
Fill a large cooking pot with enough water to cover 6 corn cobs but don't put the corn in yet. Put the pot of water over a high heat, strip the husks from the corn cobs and put half of the husks into the water. Add all of the ingredients apart from the corn and the rest of the husks, keeping the Scotch bonnet intact. Boil for a few minutes to infuse the liquid with the flavours, and then add the corn and cover with the rest of the corn husks. Bring back to the boil and boil hard for about 6 minutes. Remove the corn cobs and eat immediately.

FOLK STORY OF THE MONTH

Gang Gang Sarah – a story from Trinidad and Tobago

This story speaks of the longing for home felt among the slaves and of the impossibility of return to Africa, and even to their former idea of themselves, once they had arrived in the West Indies. Having tasted the salt of their adopted home, they were transformed, and there was no going back.

One stormy night a witch named Sarah was blown across the sea from Africa to Tobago, and landed quite neatly in the village of Les Coteaux. Her family had long before been transported there in slave ships, and Sarah had come to look for them in Golden Lane, near Les Coteaux, as she was desperate to take care of them. Although she didn't find them, she decided to stay and help the people out. She was wise and kind and she knew which herbs to give to the people for which ailments, and what potion a woman could use to make a man fall in love with her. She took care of the pregnant women and acted as midwife, which earned her the name 'Gang Gang Sarah', and she was even asked to name some of the children.

Sarah married a man called Tom, whom she had known as a child in Africa, and together they lived to a ripe old age. When Tom died, Sarah decided that it was time to fly home. She climbed to the highest limbs of a silk cotton tree and jumped. But sadly she had lost her powers of flight, having tasted the salt of her new home, which, of course, no witch must do if they hope to keep their powers intact. She fell to the ground and died, and was buried next to Tom in the plantation cemetery, where their headstones can still be seen to this day.

The tree Gang Gang Sarah is said to have fallen from is the largest of its kind on Tobago, and for many years a sign alongside it read, 'This silk cotton tree was considered sacred by the African slaves who believed that the spirits of their ancestors lived in its branches.'

FOLK SONG OF THE MONTH

'Mangoes'
Traditional, arr. Richard Barnard

Calypso was the original music of the Notting Hill Carnival, and even now the climax of the UK calypso year is the Calypso Monarch Finals, always held on the Thursday before Carnival. The style is likely descended from West African Kaiso and Canboulay songs that were sung in the plantations as a method of communication when slaves were not allowed to speak to each other. It very literally arrived in Britain with the Windrush generation: when the HMT *Empire Windrush* first arrived at London's Tilbury Docks from the Caribbean on 21st June 1948, several well-known calypsonians were

on board. A Pathé News camera filmed 'king of calypso'
Lord Kitchener singing 'London Is the Place for Me' as he
disembarked. 'Mangoes' is a Trinidadian folk song, sung to a
calypso beat and with lyrics in a mixture of Creole, English
and French, as reflects the island's heritage. No less than eight
types of mango are listed in the two verses.

Mangoes, mangoes, mangoes!
Mango vert, mango teen,
Mango vert, mango teen,
I want a penny to buy
Mango vert, mango teen.
Give me a penny to buy
Mango vert, mango teen.
Mango doodou, sousay-matin
Savez-vous all for me
Mango doodou, sousay-matin
Savez-vous all for me.

Mangoes, mangoes, mangoes!
Mango rose, mango starch,
Mango rose, mango starch,
I want a penny to buy
Mango rose, mango starch.
Give me a penny to buy
Mango rose, mango starch.
Mango zapico, calabash
Savez-vous all for me
Mango zapico, calabash
Savez-vous all for me.

A

September

1   Start of meteorological autumn

11   Enkutatash – Ethiopian New Year (Rastafarian)

23   Autumn equinox – start of astronomical autumn

23   Mabon – harvest celebration (neopagan)

25   Pearly Kings and Queens Society Harvest Festival at Guildhall Yard and parade to St Mary-le-Bow, London

25   25th–27th: Rosh Hashanah – Jewish New Year, start of Hebrew year 5783, begins at sundown

29   Michaelmas Day (Christian, traditional)

DRESSING UP IN SEPTEMBER

Horned men of the Abbots Bromley Horn Dance

The village of Abbots Bromley in Staffordshire, including the surrounding farms within the parish, is the site of one of the oldest existing folk ceremonies, the Horn Dance. It is held on Wakes Monday (the first Monday after the first Sunday after 4th September, which is 12th September this year, but check the date before you go). At 08.00 the 12 members of the troupe will set out: six Deermen, each bearing a set of horns, Maid Marian (a man in costume), a Fool, a Hobby Horse, an Archer, plus an accordionist and a triangle player. The troupe walks from farm to farm and on arrival forms into a snaking line and then does a perfunctory dance to a simple tune such as 'Yankee Doodle'. The dance entails the horned men forming two lines and stepping towards and away from each other to the music.

The horns are three sets of white and three of black reindeer antlers. Kept in the church year-round and brought out for the day, they are quite a mystery. They have been carbon-dated to around 1065, a time when reindeer were probably extinct in the British Isles, so they were likely brought over from Scandinavia. The earliest confirmed date for the Horn Dance is some time in the 1520s, though some claim that it has been going since 1226, with a few breaks and resurrections.

What the Horn Dance means has long been a source of speculation among folklorists. Some have suggested it was a pagan fertility ritual, others that it was originally connected to the ruling dynasty of Mercia, which owned the hunting grounds that surround Abbots Bromley: could this have originated as a tradition to affirm villagers' hunting rights? Still others point out that that there are earlier records of the Hobby horse than of the horned men and that perhaps this was originally a Hobby Horse tradition but the antlers – wherever they came from and whenever they appeared – rather stole the limelight. Hobby Horses pop up in lots of English folk celebrations and have tended to be part of entertainments that collect funds for churches and for the poor. Whatever it means, Abbots Bromley's Horn Dance is still going strong.

THE SKY

We have seen very little of Mars so far this year, but this month it becomes far more noticeable, appearing in the northeast at around 23.00 at the beginning of September and growing steadily earlier and brighter. Jupiter is at opposition towards the end of this month, meaning that it is in the opposite part of our sky from the sun and so a maximum amount of it is lit up, like a full moon. It will be visible high in the sky during the evening hours.

At night

11th–12th: Jupiter and the moon in conjunction. They will rise together at around 20.00 in the east and be visible all night, reaching a maximum altitude of 34 degrees at 02.00 in the south. They will be lost in the dawn at 06.00 on the 12th in the southwest at an altitude of 20 degrees.

26th–27th: Jupiter at opposition. It will be visible from 19.30 in the east until 06.30 on the 27th in the west. It will be at its maximum altitude of 38 degrees in the south at midnight.

By day

21st: At solar noon (approximately 13.00 BST/IST) the sun will reach an altitude of 38 degrees in the London sky and 34 degrees in the Glasgow sky.

23rd: The autumn equinox falls at 02.03, the moment at which the centre of the sun is directly above the equator, and so day and night are nearly of equal length all around the globe. The equinox occurs twice a year, once in March and once in September.

1st–30th: Day length decreases this month by 2h 7m in Clitheroe, Lancashire.

S

Sunrise and set
Clitheroe, Lancashire

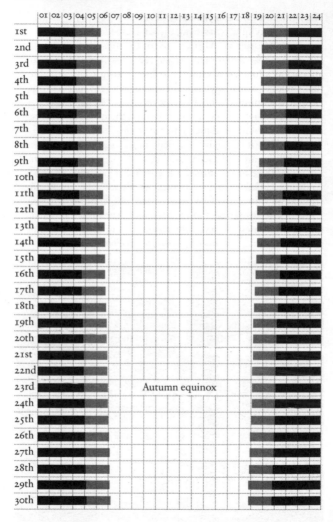

Deep-sky objects

The Andromeda Galaxy/Messier 31

At 2.5 million light years away, the Andromeda Galaxy, also known as Messier 31 (M31), is one of the most distant deep-sky objects that the human eye can see – a swirling spiral that appears as a fuzzy, oval cloud. A trillion stars are contained in that smudge, which stretches about 220,000 light years across. Despite the unimaginably vast distance between us, this is the nearest major galaxy to ours. In fact, the two galaxies are expected to collide and merge in four to five billion years.

Search for it in August and September, near the eastern horizon from around 21.00, and higher as the night wears on. First, find the constellations of Pegasus and Cassiopeia. The Andromeda Galaxy is a white smudge between the two, located straight up from two of Pegasus's stars, Mu Andromedae and Mirach. Once you have found it, try looking through binoculars and you may pick out its distinctive shape and its two satellite galaxies, Messier 32 and Messier 110, on either side of it.

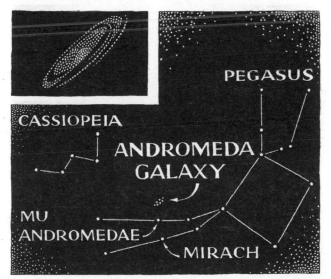

THE SEA

Average sea temperature

Shetland:	12.3°C
Greenock:	14.0°C
Cleethorpes:	15.1°C
Rhyl:	16.0°C
Rosslare:	15.2°C
Bideford:	16.8°C
Deal:	17.7°C

Spring and neap tides

Spring tides are the most extreme tides of the month, with the highest rises and the lowest falls, and they follow a couple of days after the full moon and new moon. Neap tides are the least extreme, with the smallest movement, and they fall in between the spring tides.

Spring tides: 11th–13th and 27th–29th

Neap tides: 5th–6th and 19th–20th

Spring tides are shaded in black in the chart opposite.

September tide timetable for Dover

For guidance on how to convert this for your local area, see page 8.

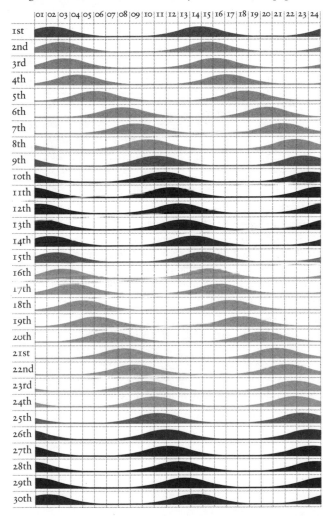

THE MOON

Moon phases

1st quarter – 3rd September, 19.07

Full moon – 10th September, 10.59

3rd quarter – 17th September, 22.52

New moon – 25th September, 22.54

Full moon
Names for September's full moon: Harvest Moon, Wine Moon, Song Moon.

The harvest moon is always the full moon that falls nearest to the autumn equinox. It can be a particularly golden moon when seen near the horizon, viewed through the dusty atmosphere of late summer.

New moon
September's new moon on the 25th is in Libra. Astrologers believe that the new moon is a good time to make plans and focus on your dreams and hopes for the period ahead, and that each new moon has a particular energy, depending on which zodiacal sign it is in. Libra is an especially harmonious sign and so it could be a good time for setting into motion tasks that require diplomacy and delicate negotiation.

Moon phases for September

1st	2nd	3rd	4th	5th
6th	7th	8th	9th	10th FULL
11th	12th	13th	14th	15th
16th	17th	18th	19th	20th
21st	22nd	23rd	24th	25th NEW
26th	27th	28th	29th	30th

THE GARDEN

Gardening by the moon

The harvest moon is the full moon closest to the autumn equinox, and it falls on 10th September this year. Harvest is one of the biggest agricultural jobs of the year, and the harvest moon traditionally allowed it to carry on beyond daylight hours. There is certainly plenty to harvest, with much of it needing to be put away for winter. There is also seed sowing, bulb planting and plant splitting to be done: a busy month after the lull of August. The weather in September can often start off as golden as the harvest moon, but the days are noticeably shortening – the autumn equinox falls on 23rd September and from then on we are into the dark half of the year.

Whether you are gardening in time with the moon or not, use the following as a guide to jobs to do in September.

Note: Sometimes these dates differ from those in the moon phase chart on page 191, to take into account sensible gardening hours. Where no specific time for the change between phases is mentioned, this is because it happens early in the morning or late at night. For exact changeover times for any late-night or pre-dawn gardening, refer to the moon phase chart.

New moon to 1st quarter: 27th August–3rd and 26th–2nd October
Rising vitality and upward growth. Plant and sow anything that develops above ground towards the end of phase. Prepare for growth.
- You can sow, plant out or take cuttings of all of those things mentioned in the next moon phase, but towards the end of this phase is better.

1st quarter to full moon: 4th–10th
Sow crops that develop above ground, don't sow root crops. Plant out seedlings and young plants. Take cuttings and make grafts. Avoid other pruning. Fertilise.
- Sow hardy annual flowers where you want them to bloom next year.

- Sow salad leaves – mustard greens, mizuna, mibuna, pak choi and chop suey greens, as well as kale, rocket, lettuces and Swiss chard – and cover with cloches.
- Sow sweet peas in the greenhouse or cold frame.
- Compost summer bedding once it is over and plant winter bedding – foliage, pansies, violas and heathers – in pots and hanging baskets.
- Plant out wallflowers for a spring display.
- Take cuttings of scented geraniums to overwinter indoors.

Full moon to 3rd quarter: 11th–17th

A 'drawing down' energy. Sow and plant crops that develop below ground: root crops, bulbs and perennials.

- Plant autumn bulbs, daffodils in particular.
- Plant up forced hyacinth bulbs and paperwhites from late September to early October for Christmas flowers.
- Plant onion sets.
- Plant new perennials in your flower borders and lift, divide and replant those that have finished flowering.

3rd quarter to new moon: 18th–25th

A dormant period, with low sap and poor growth. Do not sow or plant. Prune, weed and harvest crops for storage. Fertilise and mulch. Garden maintenance.

- Lift maincrop potatoes for storage.
- Pick apples and pears for storage. Wrap individually and place in crates.
- Once a tomato plant has produced four or five tresses of tomatoes (six or seven on some types of cherry tomatoes), 'stop' the plant by nipping out the tip.
- Deadhead dahlias to prolong flowering.
- Order spring bulbs.
- Stop feeding houseplants this month and reduce watering towards the end of the month.
- Bring tender plants inside towards the end of the month.
- Save seed from favourite flowers and crops.

S

NATURE

Birds of the month – waders

This is the best month to visit estuaries, as they become filled with birds feeding up before migrating south or arriving from the north to escape the colder months ahead. Waders frequent wetlands and the coast – their long legs and beak allow them to keep their body dry when in shallow water, and to penetrate into mud and sand for worms and insects. Three of our best-known waders are the curlew, redshank and oystercatcher.

The curlew is the largest. It has a long, down-curved beak, brown speckled colouring and a white underside. Curlews that have summered in Scotland may fly south to the English west coast and to Ireland for winter. They have a gentle, whistling flight call, which sounds very like their name. The call is associated with bad luck if you hear it at night, while sailors once believed that hearing it by day meant a storm was brewing and that they shouldn't set sail.

One of the smaller waders, the redshank is identified by its bright red legs and beak, set off by its brown speckled body with a paler underside. Redshanks will be moving now from their summer breeding grounds to estuaries and mudflats. They have a quivering hanging flight, during which they sing their song, a low-pitched 'tyu-lu-lu'. The redshank is also known as the 'sentinel of the marshes' for its panicky nature, alarm call and flight, which will be set off by any disturbance.

The oystercatcher is a large bird, with strong black and white colouring and pink legs, red eyes and a long orange bill. It is a common sight in estuaries and marshlands, as well as on beaches and rocky coasts, and some areas see huge winter gatherings – the largest is at Morecambe Bay in Lancashire, where around 41,000 birds spend the winter. In addition to resident birds, a great number will fly in from the Faroe Islands, where they are the national bird. Faroe Islanders expect them to leave on the 16th September and arrive back on the 12th March, Graekarismessa, St Gregory's Day, a timetable to which the birds apparently adhere.

OYSTERCATCHER

REDSHANK

CURLEW

THE KITCHEN

A gardener shouldn't go hungry in September. The neopagans call the autumn equinox Mabon, and believe that it was once considered the second harvest festival of the year, this one celebrating fruits. All the crops of the greenhouse are reaching their peak, while those out-of-doors are still producing and the roots and brassicas of winter are starting to mature. Oysters are now in season, the countryside is productive, hunting season for grouse and venison has begun, and hedgerows are dripping with rosehips, hazelnuts, elderberries and bullaces.

In season

In the hedgerows, woods and fields
Wild fruits and nuts: Bilberries, blackberries, crab apples, elderberries, haws, juniper berries, rosehips, rowan berries, cobnuts, hazelnuts, bullace/wild damson, walnuts
Edible wild flowers: Meadowsweet, nasturtiums (flowers and seeds)
Roots: Alexanders, dandelion, horseradish, Jerusalem artichokes, lovage, rampion, wild garlic
Game: Hare, rabbit, grouse, venison, wood pigeon

From the seashore and rivers
Fish and shellfish: Eel, mussels, oysters, black bream, brown crab, herring, lobster, mackerel, turbot, scallops, hake, megrim sole, sardines, salmon
Sea buckthorn

From the kitchen garden
Fruits: Apples, pears, loganberries, autumn raspberries, blackberries, plums, redcurrants
Vegetables: Tomatoes, aubergines, chillies, sweet peppers, runner beans, French beans, peas, beetroot, calabrese, cabbages, carrots, cauliflowers, chard, courgettes, cucumbers, endive, fennel, garlic, kale, leeks, lettuces, onions, spring onions, shallots, swedes, sweetcorn, Oriental leaves, pumpkins, winter squashes, wild rocket, spinach, turnips
Herbs: Basil, mint, dill, oregano, thyme, marjoram

From the farms
Goose, cobnuts

RECIPES

Biscuit of the month

Hazelnut and oat cookies
This knobbly biscuit makes good use of the hazelnuts now ripening in the hedgerows, if you can get to them before the squirrels.

Makes 12–15
Ingredients
90g butter
90g golden caster sugar
50g golden syrup
50g self-raising flour
Pinch of salt
125g porridge oats
50g sultanas
50g blanched and toasted hazelnuts, roughly chopped

Method
Preheat the oven to 180°C, Gas Mark 4. Line a baking sheet with nonstick baking paper. Put the butter, sugar and golden syrup in a large saucepan and heat until the butter has melted and the sugar has dissolved, stirring often. Remove from the heat. Tip in the rest of the ingredients and stir well. Scoop out 2 teaspoons of the mixture and place on the baking sheet, shaping it into a round and then flattening it. Put 7 or 8 such rounds onto the tray, spaced well apart, because they will spread as they cook. Bake for 15–17 minutes, cool on the tray for a few minutes and then move to a cooling rack. Repeat with the second batch.

S

Venison sausages and white beans with cider, cream and mustard

A pot to warm body and soul as the nights start to cool.

Serves 4
Ingredients
50g butter
1 onion, halved and thinly sliced
2 x 400g cans cannellini beans, drained
300ml cider
300ml double cream
1 bay leaf
2 sprigs thyme
8 venison sausages
Extra virgin olive oil, for frying
2 teaspoons Dijon mustard
Salt and pepper

Method

Melt the butter in a frying pan and cook the onions until soft and caramelised. Add the beans and stir to heat through. Stir in the cider, cream, bay leaf and thyme. Bring to the boil, then reduce the heat and leave to simmer for 30 minutes.

Meanwhile, fry the sausages in oil in another pan for 15–20 minutes until browned and cooked through. When you are ready to serve, add the mustard to the beans and season. Make a mound of beans on each plate and place the sausages on top.

FOLK SONG OF THE MONTH

'The Hunt Is Up'
Traditional, arr. Richard Barnard

In honour of the possible – if unlikely – link between the
Horn Dance of Abbots Bromley, the nearby former hunting
grounds of Cannock Chase and ancient Needwood Forest,
and the legend of Herne the Hunter, here is a hunting song.
It is attributed to William Gray, a 16th-century ballad writer
and Member of Parliament who attracted the notice of Henry
VIII with this ballad.

The hunt is up, the hunt is up and it is near-ly day, and
Har-ry our king is a-way to bring his ro-yal deer to bay.

The hunt is up, the hunt is up
And it is nearly day,
And Harry our king is away to bring
His royal deer to bay.

The east is bright with morning light
And darkness it is fled,
A merry horn wakes up the morn
To leave his idle bed.

The horses snort to be at sport,
The dogs are running free,
The woods rejoice at the merry noise
Of 'Hey Taranta Tee Ree!'

Awake all men, I say again,
Be merry as you may,
And Harry our king is away to bring
His royal deer to bay.

FOLK STORY OF THE MONTH

Herne the Hunter

We are into deer-hunting season now, and so here is a tale of one of the greatest hunters ever known, turned vengeful spirit of the forest.

Herne was the head forester of Richard II in the 14th century, with dominion over the Windsor Castle royal forest and hunting park. His skills were immense: his arrow was true, he could anticipate every move the deer would make, and he was a great horseman, riding like a gale blowing through the ancient trees. He was also handsome, tall and sturdy like an oak, and the king favoured him greatly.

This made the other foresters jealous, and one moonless night they met in the forest to plot against him. As they gathered, a stranger appeared on a large black steed. They couldn't see his face, but in a deep voice he said, 'I will help to stop this man who has stolen the king's affections, and ask in return only that you each grant me one request when the deed is done.' Too cowardly to deal with Herne themselves, the men agreed, despite their foreboding.

The next day, when the king called the men together for the hunt, Herne was saddled up and ready to go. But as they set off, his horse reared and bucked and crashed into the king's steed. Throughout the hunt Herne lagged behind, never taking the lead, and when he was called upon to finish off a tired stag, he missed his mark. This continued over the weeks that followed: Herne had lost his skills, and the king dismissed him from his post. Heartbroken, Herne walked deep into the forest and hanged himself from an oak tree.

Soon rumours began of a terrifying woodland spirit seen in the forest. He looked like Herne, was as tall, broad and skilful as Herne, but had a great pair of antlers sprouting from his head. Now the foresters were scared, and soon the stranger appeared to them again. He told them that when Herne appeared before them, they were to obey his every command, and that he would take the immortal soul of any that didn't. Almost immediately, Herne appeared. He made them meet him by the oak at midnight and then led them on a hunt through the night, only letting them crawl home to their beds as dawn broke. This he commanded night after night, until the men were so exhausted and useless that they confessed all to the king, who had them executed.

Herne's oak was blown down in 1863, but Queen Victoria had it replaced with a new oak on the same spot. That tree was removed in 1906 but yet another oak was planted in its place and today bears the title of Herne's Oak. Even now, those who live around the forest hear the sound of hunting horns at midnight, and some have even glimpsed a ghostly hunt chasing through the moonlit trees.

S

October

1 Start of English pudding season

1 Start of Black History Month

2 Pearly Kings and Queens of St Pancras Harvest Festival at St Martin-in-the-Fields, London

4 4th–5th: Yom Kippur – Day of Atonement (Jewish), begins at sundown

7 Prophet Muhammad's birthday (Muslim), begins at sundown

9 First day of Tabernacles/Sukkot (Jewish), begins at sundown

21 Apple Day

24 Diwali – festival of lights (Hindu/Sikh/Jain)

30 British Summer Time and Irish Standard Time end – clocks go back one hour at 02.00

31 Hallowe'en

31 October bank holiday, Ireland

DRESSING UP IN OCTOBER

Pearly Kings and Queens

On the first Sunday in October (the 2nd this year), the Pearly Kings and Queens of St Pancras hold their Harvest Festival at St Martin-in-the-Fields. Another Pearly Harvest Festival is held in late September at the Guildhall Yard and St Mary-le-Bow (see page 183). Both are great gatherings of Pearlies in all their finery.

Harvest and fresh produce are at the core of Pearly history. Their story begins with the costermongers, who have traded in London for up to a thousand years. The word comes from Costard, a widely available variety of apple in medieval times, and monger, which meant 'seller'. In fact, these traders sold all sorts of fresh produce in the streets and alleyways, first from barrows and later from market stalls, mostly serving the poor who could only afford to buy in small amounts and wouldn't have been welcomed in the shops. They hawked their wares with distinctive cries, much to the annoyance of well-to-do society, and became known for their style and panache, their use of slang and their love of ale houses, gin palaces and music halls – cosy places to be when lodgings were so often grim.

Costermongers were often unlicensed, itinerant traders, and despite the essential service they provided, were much harassed by the authorities. As London grew, the costermongers elected a 'coster king' and often a 'coster queen' from each borough to fight for their rights – a sort of early trade union rep. The kings and queens also raised money for fellow costermongers who had fallen on hard times, and for the London poor they saw all around them. In time, the 'royal' children of the coster kings and queens inherited their titles and charitable duties.

The costume came in the 1880s when road-sweeper and rat-catcher Henry Croft, a friend and admirer of the costers, found a stash of smoked pearl buttons and used them to decorate a worn-out suit and top hat with the words 'All For Charity'. The costers loved to wear pearls to emulate the clothing of wealthy West End society and they quickly followed Croft's example, the women adding ostrich feathers, the men pearling working caps and waistcoats. To this day they continue to raise huge sums of money for charity, while looking very dapper indeed.

THE SKY

This month we start to see more of the winter constellations of Orion the Hunter and the Great Dog, which will both be high in the sky by the early hours of the morning. They will gradually creep around to the evening hours to keep us company all winter long. Jupiter is still bright and high in the sky, and Mars is increasing in brightness.

There will be a partial solar eclipse on the 25th, a not particularly spectacular one, with just over 15 per cent coverage, but interesting if you can find a safe way of viewing. Do not be tempted to look directly at it – you won't see anything and will damage your eyes. It's much better to make a pinhole camera (literally just a hole in a piece of card) and stand with your back to the sun, projecting the pin of light onto a piece of paper. Move the card backwards and forwards to bring it into focus and make a sharply outlined circle. This is the sun. You will then see the shadow of the moon gradually moving across it and away. It is fun to do this with a colander, and see 50-odd suns being partially eclipsed by 50-odd moons.

At night

8th–9th: Conjunction of Jupiter and the moon. They will rise together at around 18.50 in the east and will reach their maximum altitude of 43 degrees at around 02.00 in the south before setting in the west at around 05.30 on the 9th.

By day

21st: At solar noon (approximately 13.00 BST/IST) the sun will reach an altitude of 28 degrees in the London sky and 24 degrees in the Glasgow sky.
25th: Partial solar eclipse, from 10.08 to 11.51, at its maximum (of only 15 per cent sun coverage) at 10.59.
1st–31st: Day length decreases this month by 2h 9m at Clitheroe, Lancashire.

O

Sunrise and set
Clitheroe, Lancashire

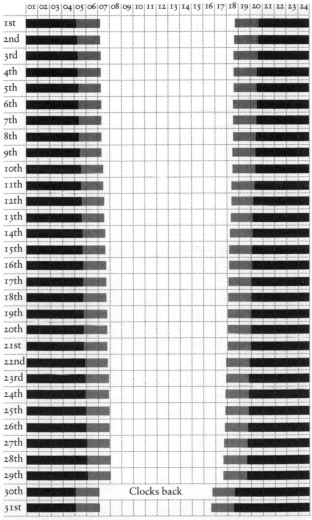

British Summer Time and Irish Standard Time end on 30th October at 02.00 and this has been accounted for above.

Deep-sky objects

The Hyades

The Hyades star cluster is so loose and bright that it makes up a major part of the constellation Taurus. Its primary stars – Gamma, Delta 1, Epsilon and Theta Tauri – form the head of the bull along with bright Aldebaran. Aldebaran is unrelated and lies closer to earth, but falls along the same line of sight.

The Hyades is the nearest open cluster of stars to the solar system, a mere 153 light years away. About 15 of its stars are visible to the naked eye, and binoculars or a telescope will reveal at least 30 more. It is similar in make-up and trajectory to the Beehive Cluster (see page 57) and appears to have come from the same region of the sky, which suggests a common origin.

Together with the nearby Pleiades (see page 227), the Hyades make up the Golden Gate of the Ecliptic, each of them a post either side of the ecliptic, which is the apparent circular path along which the sun travels through our skies in a year.

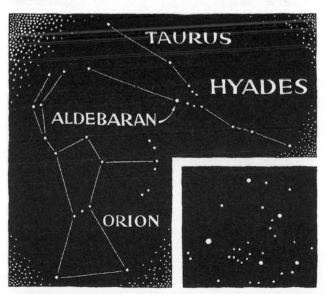

O

THE SEA

Average sea temperature

Shetland:	11.4°C
Greenock:	13.2°C
Cleethorpes:	13.0°C
Rhyl:	14.4°C
Rosslare:	14.1°C
Bideford:	15.3°C
Deal:	16.1°C

Spring and neap tides

Spring tides are the most extreme tides of the month, with the highest rises and the lowest falls, and they follow a couple of days after the full moon and new moon. Neap tides are the least extreme, with the smallest movement, and they fall in between the spring tides.

Spring tides: 10th–12th and 26th–28th

Neap tides: 4th–5th and 18th–19th

Spring tides are shaded in black in the chart opposite.

October tide timetable for Dover

For guidance on how to convert this for your local area, see page 8.

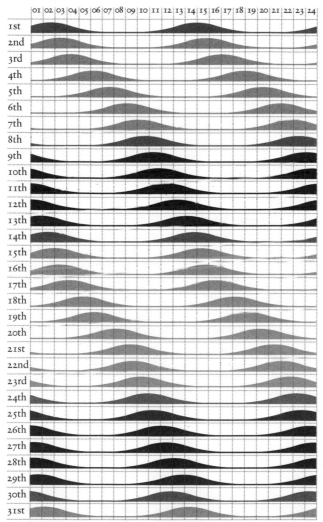

British Summer Time and Irish Standard Time end on 30th October at 02.00, and this has been accounted for above.

THE MOON

Moon phases

1st quarter – 3rd October, 01.14

Full moon – 9th October, 21.54

3rd quarter – 17th October, 18.15

New moon – 25th October, 11.48

Full moon
Names for October's full moon: Hunter's Moon, Blood Moon.

New moon
The new moon is in Scorpio. Astrologers believe that the new moon is a good time to make plans and focus on your dreams and hopes for the period ahead, and that each new moon has a particular energy, depending on which zodiacal sign it is in. Scorpio is intense and sensual, so this would be a good time to begin working on personal empowerment and the fulfilment of your deepest desires.

Moon phases for October

1st	2nd	3rd	4th	5th

6th	7th	8th	9th FULL	10th

11th	12th	13th	14th	15th

16th	17th	18th	19th	20th

21st	22nd	23rd	24th	25th NEW

26th	27th	28th	29th	30th

31st				

O

THE GARDEN

Gardening by the moon

The temperature is dropping and the leaves are changing. This month will see the clocks go back on the 30th: an abrupt end to the gentle slide into the darker months. It would be quite usual to have a first frost by the end of the month, though St Luke's Day on the 18th is said to often herald 'St Luke's little summer': a few days of late, fine weather. Everything vulnerable is being put away, with perennials dying back to their roots, trees shedding their leaves, and animals tucking away supplies or going into hibernation. We must do the same, putting away tender plants and harvesting crops for storage.

Whether you are gardening in time with the moon or not, use the following as a guide to jobs to do in October.

Note: Sometimes these dates differ from those in the moon phase chart on page 211, to take into account sensible gardening hours. Where no specific time for the change between phases is mentioned, this is because it happens early in the morning or late at night. For exact changeover times for any late-night or pre-dawn gardening, refer to the moon phase chart.

New moon to 1st quarter: 26th September–2nd and 25th (from 11.48)–31st

Rising vitality and upward growth. Plant and sow anything that develops above ground towards the end of phase. Prepare for growth.

- You can sow, plant out or take cuttings of all of those things mentioned in the next moon phase, but towards the end of this phase is better.

1st quarter to full moon: 3rd–9th

Sow crops that develop above ground, don't sow root crops. Plant out seedlings and young plants. Take cuttings and make grafts. Avoid other pruning. Fertilise.

- Sow sweet peas and hardy varieties of pea in pots in the greenhouse or cold frame.

- Sow broad beans, direct or in pots in the greenhouse.
- Plant out wallflowers, violas, forget-me-nots and other spring bedding.

Full moon to 3rd quarter: 10th–17th
A 'drawing down' energy. Sow and plant crops that develop below ground: root crops, bulbs and perennials.
- Plant up hyacinth, paperwhite and hippeastrum bulbs in early October for Christmas flowers.
- Plant spring bulbs – last chance for daffodils, perfect timing for crocuses, scilla, fritillaries and irises.
- Plant lilies and ornamental alliums.
- Plant garlic cloves and overwintering onion sets.
- Plant rhubarb crowns and bare-root fruit bushes.
- Plant new grapevines, peaches and nectarines.
- Plant new herbaceous perennials, and lift, divide and replant those that are over.

3rd quarter to new moon: 18th–25th (till 11.48)
A dormant period, with low sap and poor growth. Do not sow or plant. Prune, weed and harvest crops for storage. Fertilise and mulch. Garden maintenance.
- Lift maincrop potatoes and prepare them for storage.
- Lift and store beetroot and turnips before the ground freezes. Leave carrots and parsnips until needed.
- Cut pumpkins and winter squashes on a fine day and leave to 'cure' in the sun for a few days for better storage.
- Pick apples and pears for storage. Wrap individually in paper and place in crates.
- Cover salad leaves and leafy vegetables with cloches.
- Dismantle and store supports for runner beans, peas and tomatoes.
- Pick green tomatoes for chutney or put into paper bags in a dark place where they can ripen slowly.
- Deadhead dahlias to prolong flowering.
- Earth up Brussels sprouts and other brassicas and earth up leeks.

O

THE KITCHEN

With the drop in temperature and light this month, our appetites turn to the rich and comforting: stews, roasts, pies and crumbles. And towards the end of the month, we have the great frenzy of sweet eating with Diwali and Hallowe'en.

In season

In the hedgerows, woods and fields
Wild fruits and nuts: Bullace/wild damsons, crab apples, elderberries, haws, juniper berries, rose, rowan berries, sloes, hazelnuts, sweet chestnuts, walnuts
Fungi: Ceps, chanterelles, field mushrooms, horse mushrooms, common puffballs, parasols, shaggy inkcaps
Roots: Alexanders, dandelion, horseradish, Jerusalem artichokes, lovage, rampion, wild garlic
Wild greens: Chickweed, hairy bittercress, dandelion leaves, sow thistle, wintercress/yellow rocket, sorrel
Game: Pheasant, grouse, goose, hare, mallard, rabbit, venison

From the seashore and rivers
Fish and shellfish: Black bream, herring, lobster, mackerel, turbot, eels, oysters, hake, lemon sole, sardines
Sea buckthorn

From the kitchen garden
Fruits: Medlars, quinces, apples, pears
Vegetables: Aubergines, chillies, sweet peppers, beetroot, Brussels sprouts, cabbages, carrots, cauliflowers, celeriac, celery, chard, chicory, endive, fennel, garlic, kale, leeks, lettuces, onions, Oriental leaves, parsnips, potatoes, salsify, scorzonera, spinach, spring onions, swedes, tomatoes, turnips, winter squashes
Herbs: Chervil, parsley, coriander, sage, rosemary, bay

And traditional imports
Truffles, Vacherin Mont d'Or

RECIPES

Biscuit of the month

Witch's fingers
A genuinely gruesome-looking biscuit for Hallowe'en.

Makes 10
Ingredients
50g butter, softened
50g caster sugar
1 egg yolk
¼ teaspoon almond extract
Few drops of green food colouring
40g ground almonds
100g plain flour
Pinch of salt
10 blanched almonds
3 tablespoons strawberry or raspberry jam

Method
Preheat the oven to 190C°, Gas Mark 5. Line a baking sheet with nonstick baking paper. Cream the butter with the sugar until light and fluffy and then add the egg yolk, almond extract and food colouring. Beat until incorporated. Mix in the ground almonds, flour and salt to form a dough, then knead briefly and tip out onto a lightly floured surface.

Shape the dough into a log and cut into 10 pieces. Roll each piece into a long, finger-like shape tapered at one end. Lay on the baking sheet. Add a small blob of jam to one end and then press an almond over the jam to make a nail. Use the end of a knife to flatten the other 'severed' end. Use the knife blade to make 3 parallel lines at each knuckle. Squeeze the gaps between the knuckles to make the fingers look bony.

Bake for 12–14 minutes and cool on a wire rack. When they are cool, dip the severed ends into the remaining jam and arrange on a serving plate.

O

Leek pudding

The 1st October is the start of the English pudding season. As fun as this sounds, the original puddings were a way of using up the parts of an animal that were hard to preserve. Livestock was slaughtered in October and November to save on animal feed over the winter, and so there would have been a lot of meat to preserve and offal to deal with.

Here is a hearty example of what the pudding evolved into. This is a traditional savoury pudding from the northeast of England, and it was served sliced with meat and gravy. Leftovers sliced and fried in butter on the next day, then topped with a runny fried egg, are even better.

Serves 4
Ingredients
225g plain flour
1 teaspoon salt
1 teaspoon baking powder
100g shredded suet
450g leeks, finely chopped
8–10 tablespoons water

Method
Grease a 1.2-litre pudding bowl. In a mixing bowl, stir together the flour, salt, baking powder and suet. Add the leeks and mix well, then add enough of the water to form a sticky dough. Tip into the pudding bowl. Cover with a piece of nonstick baking paper, giving it a little pleat by folding it in half and then folding it back on itself for 2–3cm. Secure by tying string around the rim. Put an upturned plate on the base of a large saucepan and pour in about 8cm of boiling water. Place the bowl on top of the plate then pour in more boiling water to halfway up the bowl. Bring to the boil, then reduce to a simmer, cover and steam for 3 hours, checking the water level occasionally and topping up as necessary. Serve hot with gravy.

FOLK STORY OF THE MONTH

The Peddler of Swaffham

The peddler in this story does not take his wares to London, but he finds his fortune there anyway, in a roundabout way.

There was once a poor peddler who lived in Swaffham in Norfolk. Every day he would buy produce from the market gardens and pick apples from his own orchard, and then hawk them in the streets and marketplace. One night he had a vivid dream that he was standing on London Bridge. This was in the days when London Bridge was lined with shops from one end to the other, and in the dream he was surrounded by noise and bustle. As he stood outside a haberdasher's shop on the bridge, he was told the most wonderful news. But when he woke up he could no longer remember what it was. The following night he had the dream again, and the next night he had it yet again. When he woke on the third morning, he decided he had to walk to London and see if he could find out what this news might be.

When he arrived at London Bridge, all looked just as it had in his dream. He heard the cries of the costermongers – 'Penny a lot, fine russets!' and 'Four bunches a penny: water cresses'. He walked up and down the bridge all day long, but he was none the wiser. The next day he did the same, with the same result. On the third day a shopkeeper stepped out of his haberdashery shop and hailed him. 'I have seen you walking here these past few days,' said the shopkeeper. 'You have no goods to sell and you are not begging. What is your business?' The peddler told him about his dream, at which the shopkeeper laughed. 'You are a fool to come all this way because of a dream,' he said. 'Why, I too have had a dream every night for the past week, that there is a pot of gold hidden under an apple tree in a town called Swaffham that I have never visited and never intend to visit. Be off home with you!' The peddler did exactly as he was told, and walked all the way home. In his orchard he dug up the gold, which kept him in fine style for the rest of his days.

FOLK SONG OF THE MONTH

'The Costermonger's Song'
Traditional, arr. Richard Barnard

The costermongers (see page 204), were known for their vibrant pub culture. The original Music Hall venues of the 1830s were 'song and supper rooms' in the salon bars of public houses. Created so that the working classes could eat, drink and smoke while being entertained, they were very different from the more genteel, middle-class theatres. Many of the songs were bawdy and rousing, written to be sung along to at top volume. 'Coster songs' such as this were sung in an exaggerated Cockney accent, and often featured mentions of the wares they sold.

Swing ♩ = 120

I'm Bil-ly Bell, a cos-ter-mon-ger-er, you sees, a-sell-ing of po-ta-toes,

leeks and cab-ba ges,__ ar-ti-chokes and cau-li-flowers; I thinks that I can say I

deals in ev-ery-thing what's in the ve-ge-ta-ble way.__ And

though I work so ve-ry hard I has me plea-sure too, for ev-ery Der-by Day a-way to

Ep-som I would go. *Go-ing to the Der-by look-ing ve-ry smart,*

do-ing all the jour-ney in me donk-ey cart. Pass-ing all the vehi-cles,

turn-ing in and out, go-ing to the Der-by in me lit-tle donk-ey cart.

I'm Billy Bell, a coster-monger, you sees,
A-selling of potatoes, leeks and cabbages,
Artichokes and cauliflowers; I thinks that I can say
I deals in everything what's in the vegetable way.
And though I work so very hard, I has me pleasure too
For every Derby Day away to Epsom I would go.

Going to the Derby looking very smart,
Doing all the journey in me donkey cart.
Passing all the vehicles, turning in and out,
Going to the Derby in me little donkey cart.

And when I gets to Epsom amongst the bustle there
I puts away me donkey what hasn't turned a hair.
Then I gets me luncheon: a chunk of bread and cheese,
A gallon jar of fourpenny, at which you wouldn't sneeze.
And if I've won a bob or two, I has an happy heart
Returning from the Derby in my little donkey cart.

Going to the Derby looking very smart,
Doing all the journey in me donkey cart.
Passing all the vehicles, turning in and out,
Going to the Derby in me little donkey cart.

O

NATURE

Bird of the month – house sparrow

'Incessant' is the best way to describe the noise a group of sparrows makes. If you are lucky enough to have them in your garden or nesting in your eaves, you will know that they come as a gang, and they can be riotously noisy all year round. The song is not musical in the slightest. An endless cheeping and chirping as if they have way too much to say to each other, it is a joyous racket, made by these stout, confident, cheeky little birds.

House sparrows love to be around humans, and so they are found wherever we are found. They are opportunistic feeders that do well off our scraps and waste, and, of course, from our bird feeders, too, but they also make their colonies of nests in the eaves of older houses. So comfortable are they in large cities that they have become synonymous with London, 'my old cock sparrow', 'my old cocker', 'my old cock' – referring to a male sparrow – being a Cockney phrase of endearment, usually referring to a quick and confident young man.

Despite all of this, sparrows saw a massive decline of 71 per cent between 1977 and 2008, perhaps due to the loss of gardens to paving and the smartening up and conversion of so many roof spaces. Figures have recently shown signs of a rallying, but sparrows definitely need support. Give them food and water throughout winter, and try to resist ripping out old hedges or adding plastic fascias to roofs.

Sparrows have rounded, stout bodies and chunky, triangular beaks. Males have strong markings in black, brown and grey, with a grey head and black eye stripe, and black and brown wing feathers. Females are less strongly marked, with a soft brown head and grey underside, and finer, softer brown and black wing feathers.

HOUSE SPARROW

MALE

FEMALE

November

1   Samhain, end of harvest/start of winter celebration (Gaelic/pagan/neopagan)

1   All Saints' Day (Christian)

2   All Souls' Day (Christian)

5   Guy Fawkes Night

5   Bridgwater Carnival

11   Armistice Day/Remembrance Day

11   Martinmas (Christian, traditional)

13   Remembrance Sunday

17   Beaujolais Nouveau Day

21   Stir-up Sunday

24   Thanksgiving (American)

27   First Sunday in Advent (Christian)

30   St Andrew's Day – patron saint of Scotland

DRESSING UP IN NOVEMBER

Smugglers at Lewes Bonfire Societies Bonfire Night

Guy Fawkes Night is one of the most widely celebrated events in the British calendar, and on the 5th November the dark skies will be filled with sparkles, whizzes and bangs and with the tang of smoke, sulphur and saltpetre. While most people content themselves with attending a community bonfire or a firework display, the celebrations in Lewes, Sussex, have gone in a different direction. Seven 'bonfire societies' put on costumed processions and parade spectacular papier-mâché tableaux of controversial figures of the day, typically politicians and celebrities. Each bonfire society drags flaming tar barrels through the streets of its own area of the town, ending in a fireworks display and burning the tableaux. The bonfire societies each have two sets of costumes that their members wear every year. Themes include buccaneers, monks, Tudors, Vikings, French revolutionaries, ancient Greeks – and 'smugglers', who wear striped jumpers in colours that identify their society, with white trousers, black boots, and often a hat or a bandana.

The origins of this event were chaotic. The 5th November was one night when wild behaviour and civil disobedience were overlooked by the police, and over time it developed into a night of riots and protest by 'Bonfire Boys' against the authorities. Two centuries ago, one of the main points of disgruntlement came from men who had returned from the Napoleonic Wars to destitution. They formed into gangs based in the seaports of England's south coast, adopting the French striped sailor shirts known as *marinières*, as these allowed them to operate as a unit and avoid individual identification. Different gangs wore different-coloured stripes.

The bonfires and the burning of the effigies became a way of expressing their disgust at the establishment, and flaming barrels were rolled down the wealthy and commercial streets of Lewes to threaten businesses and show the Bonfire Boys' anger. This culminated in riots in 1847, when the local police had to call in reinforcements from London. An uneasy truce led to the proper formation of the bonfire societies, and eventually to the transformation of these 'riots' into the just-about-family-friendly annual event it is now.

THE SKY

Mars will be at opposition early next month so it is high and bright in the sky all night now, reaching its maximum height around midnight, in the south. Jupiter is still very noticeable too, becoming visible in the dusk in the southeast at around 16.30 and setting in the west at about midnight.

At night

4th–5th: Conjunction of Jupiter and the moon. They will appear in the east at around 17.00 on the 4th, reach a maximum altitude of 35 degrees in the south at around 21.00 and set at around 02.20 on the 5th in the west.

By day

21st: At solar noon the sun will reach an altitude of 18 degrees in the London sky and 14 degrees in the Glasgow sky.

1st–30th: Day length decreases this month by 1h 40m at Clitheroe, Lancashire.

N

Sunrise and set
Clitheroe, Lancashire

Deep-sky objects

The Pleiades/Seven Sisters/Messier 45

The Pleiades is one of the most beautiful deep-sky objects that you can see with the naked eye, and one of the largest, at four times the width of the full moon. It is also known as the Seven Sisters because of its seven glitteringly prominent stars but, in fact, in dark-sky conditions more can be seen, and there are over a thousand stars in the group. They are 444 light years away. The stars of the Pleiades are all related, rather than being a chance formation, and are thought to have once resembled the Orion Nebula. Find them by following the upward slope of Orion's belt, past bright Aldebaran in the constellation of Taurus. Aldebaran means 'follower' in Arabic, because it chases the Pleiades through the sky each night.

Together with the Hyades, the Pleiades make up the Golden Gate of the Ecliptic (see page 207).

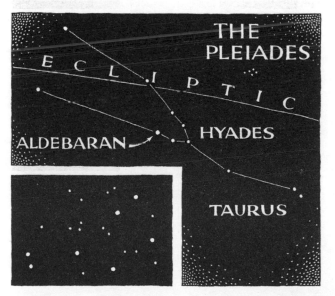

THE SEA

Average sea temperature

Shetland:	10.9°C
Greenock:	11.9°C
Cleethorpes:	10.7°C
Rhyl:	12.4°C
Rosslare:	12.9°C
Bideford:	13.7°C
Deal:	13.8°C

Spring and neap tides

Spring tides are the most extreme tides of the month, with the highest rises and the lowest falls, and they follow a couple of days after the full moon and new moon. Neap tides are the least extreme, with the smallest movement, and they fall in between the spring tides.

Spring tides: 9th–11th and 24th–26th

Neap tides: 2nd–3rd and 17th–18th

Spring tides are shaded in black in the chart opposite.

November tide timetable for Dover

For guidance on how to convert this for your local area, see page 8.

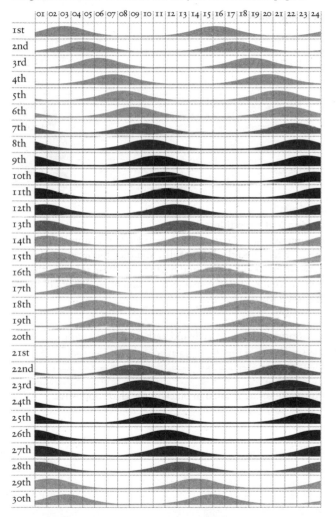

THE MOON

Moon phases

1st quarter – 1st November, 06.37

Full moon – 8th November, 11.02

3rd quarter – 16th November, 13.27

New moon – 23rd November, 22.57

1st quarter – 30th November, 14.36

Full moon

Names for November's full moon: Darkest Depths Moon, Mourning Moon.

New moon

November's new moon on the 23rd is in Sagittarius. Astrologers believe that the new moon is a good time to make plans and focus on your dreams and hopes for the period ahead, and that each new moon has a particular energy, depending on which zodiacal sign it is in. Sagittarius is a freedom-loving sign, making this a good time to plan travel or to contemplate how to release some of the bonds holding you.

At the predicted sighting of the new crescent moon on the 25th, the Jewish month of Kislev will begin. Hanukkah, the Jewish festival of lights, begins on the 24th day of Kislev (18th December this year).

Moon phases for November

1st	2nd	3rd	4th	5th
6th	7th	8th FULL	9th	10th
11th	12th	13th	14th	15th
16th	17th	18th	19th	20th
21st	22nd	23rd NEW	24th	25th
26th	27th	28th	29th	30th

N

THE GARDEN

Gardening by the moon

November can be a beautiful month as the trees reach their full glowing autumn colour, picked up by the low winter light. But we don't want it too easy. A warm November is said to bring a cold winter. Martinmas (St Martin's Day), on 11th November, is the crucial day, as an old adage goes: 'Ice before Martinmas enough to bear a duck/The rest of winter, is sure to be but muck' – and vice versa. Whichever way it goes, it is time to finish autumn tasks and begin winter ones, such as pruning trees and taking care of the soil.

Whether you are gardening in time with the moon or not, use the following as a guide to jobs to do in November.

Note: Sometimes these dates differ from those in the moon phase chart on page 231, to take into account sensible gardening hours. Where no specific time for the change between phases is mentioned, this is because it happens early in the morning or late at night. For exact changeover times for any late-night or pre-dawn gardening, refer to the moon phase chart.

1st quarter to full moon: 1st–8th (till 11.02) and 30th (from 14.36)–7th December
Sow crops that develop above ground, don't sow root crops. Plant out seedlings and young plants. Take cuttings and make grafts. Avoid other pruning. Fertilise.
- Sow broad beans, direct into the ground or in pots in the greenhouse.
- Sow sweet peas and hardy varieties of pea in pots in the greenhouse.

Full moon to 3rd quarter: 8th (from 11.02)–16th (till 13.27)
A 'drawing down' energy. Sow and plant crops that develop below ground: root crops, bulbs and perennials.
- Plant spring bulbs: the perfect moment for tulips in particular. Plant lily and ornamental allium bulbs.
- Plant up paperwhite, miniature iris and forced hyacinth bulbs for late winter indoor flowers.

- Plant garlic cloves and overwintering onion sets.
- Plant rhubarb crowns and bare-root fruit bushes.
- Plant new grapevines, peaches and nectarines.
- Bare-root top fruit is now available: plant apples, pears, quinces and medlar.
- Plant new perennials. Lift, divide and replant those that are over.

3rd quarter to new moon: 16th (from 13.27)–23rd

A dormant period, with low sap and poor growth. Do not sow or plant. Prune, weed and harvest crops for storage. Fertilise and mulch. Garden maintenance.

- Prune apple, pear, medlar and quince trees.
- Prune grapevines before the winter solstice.
- Remove nets from fruit cages. Prune autumn-fruiting raspberries, red and white currants, and gooseberries.
- Remove unripened figs.
- Check your soil for its pH level. If it is low add lime or calcified seaweed.
- Mulch beds with organic manure.
- Pick apples and pears for storage. Wrap individually in paper and place in crates.
- Lift dahlias once blackened by first frosts. Dry out and store the tubers in moist sand somewhere frost-free.
- Weed.
- Prune roses.
- Collect fallen leaves into leaf mould bins or bin bags. Water lightly, tie up and forget them for a year or two to make leaf mould.

New moon to 1st quarter: 24th–30th (till 14.36)

Rising vitality and upward growth. Plant and sow anything that develops above ground towards the end of phase. Prepare for growth.

- You can sow, plant out or take cuttings of all of those things mentioned in the 1st quarter to full moon phase now, but ideally towards the end of this phase.

N

THE KITCHEN

The beginning of November brings Samhain, the final Gaelic harvest festival and the start of winter. Now comes the final fling of the forager, of mushrooms, rosehips, haws and sloes.

In season

In the hedgerows, woods and fields
Wild fruits and nuts: Bullace/wild damsons, crab apples, haws, juniper berries, rosehips, rowan berries, sloes, sweet chestnuts, walnuts
Fungi: Ceps, chanterelles, field mushrooms, horse mushrooms, common puffballs, parasols, shaggy inkcaps
Roots: Alexanders, dandelion, horseradish, Jerusalem artichokes, lovage, rampion, wild garlic
Wild greens: Chickweed, hairy bittercress, dandelion leaves, sow thistle, wintercress/yellow rocket, sorrel
Game: Grouse, hare, pheasant, rabbit, venison, partridge

From the seashore and rivers
Fish and shellfish: Black bream, herring, oysters, turbot, mussels, brill, sardines, skate, clams, mussels

From the kitchen garden
Fruits: Quinces, medlars, pears
Vegetables: Cabbages, cardoons, carrots, celeriac, celery, chard, chicory, endive, kale, leeks, lettuces, onions, spring onions, shallots, Oriental leaves, parsnips, potatoes, pumpkins, winter squashes, salsify, scorzonera, spinach, swedes, turnips
Herbs: Chervil, parsley, coriander, sage, rosemary, bay

From the farms
Goose

And traditional imports
Vacherin Mont d'Or, Beaujolais nouveau, truffles, cranberries, satsumas, clementines, pomegranates

RECIPES

Biscuit of the month

Thar cake

This also goes by Thor, Tharve, Tharf and Theor cake, all from the Old English *theorf*, meaning 'unleavened': a fittingly plain name for something traditionally eaten on the solemn occasion of All Souls' Day, 2nd November. Sometimes they were thick and more like cake or flapjacks, while others were thin and more like biscuits, as here. They were often baked hard and kept as good-luck charms.

Makes about 10
Ingredients
225g fine oatmeal
2 tablespoons plain flour
2 teaspoons ground ginger
½ teaspoon baking powder
Pinch of salt
25g butter, softened
175g black treacle

Method

Preheat the oven to 180°C, Gas Mark 4. Line a baking sheet with nonstick baking paper and rub it all over with butter to grease it. In a large bowl mix the oatmeal, flour, ginger, baking powder and salt and then rub in the butter. Add the treacle and mix to form a very stiff dough, then place on a lightly floured surface and roll out to a thickness of 6mm. Cut into 5cm rounds, lay on the greased baking sheet and bake for 10–12 minutes. Allow them to cool a little on the tray to firm up, and then use a spatula to move them to a cooling rack to cool completely.

N

Beef chilli bonfire bowl

This is much more chilli con carne than *mole* (pronounced moh-lay), the national dish of Mexico, but it does contain some *mole*-like touches. Famously, *mole* contains chocolate, which brings out the richness of the spices, but this dish also steals some *mole* chilli varieties: ancho, mulato and pasilla. These take some tracking down but you can buy them online and in fancier supermarkets, and they are worth the trouble. If you can't find them, skip the chilli soaking and blending stage and just add 1–2 tablespoons chipotle paste and a little water with the tomatoes and beans. Ancho chillies are mild, mellow and fruity; mulato are fruity and chocolatey; and pasilla have a medium heat and a distinctive, liquorice flavour. This chilli is also delicious served on rice.

Serves 6
Ingredients
2 mulato, 1 ancho and 1 pasilla chillies
4 tablespoons extra virgin olive oil
1 onion, diced
5 garlic cloves, crushed or finely chopped
1 cinnamon stick
¼ teaspoon ground cloves
1 teaspoon ground coriander
1 teaspoon ground cumin
400g beef mince
2 x 400g cans chopped tomatoes
400g can black beans, drained
2 limes
50g plain dark chocolate, 85 per cent cocoa solids
130ml sour cream

Leaves from a small bunch of fresh coriander, finely chopped

Salt and pepper

Tortilla chips, to dip

Method

Cut the stems from the tops of each chilli and then slit them down their sides to release the seeds, saving the seeds for later if needed. Heat a dry frying pan over a high heat and put the chillies into the pan in batches, holding each down until the skin blisters. Remove and place in a bowl and then just cover with boiled water. Set aside.

Heat the oil in a pan and gently fry the onion until softened, about 15–20 minutes. Add the garlic and spices to the pan and cook for a few minutes, then turn up the heat, add the beef mince and cook until it is browned all over. Drain the chillies, reserving the water for later. Put them into a food processor with a little of the chilli water. Blitz, then tip them into the pan, along with the tomatoes, the beans and a little of the chilli water. Bring to the boil and then cover, turn down the heat, and simmer for 1 hour, stirring occasionally to stop it from sticking, and adding more chilli water if it needs it.

When you are ready to serve the chilli, season it with salt and pepper, add the juice of ½ lime and the chocolate, allowing it to melt before stirring it in. Transfer into 6 individual bowls, and top each one with the sour cream, a scattering of coriander, ¼ lime squeezed over and a handful of tortilla chips.

Quince and maple rice pudding

The two layers of this rice pudding are assembled separately and then baked together. Of course, you could just dollop the fruit onto the rice prior to baking, but the extra time in the oven does add more than the sum of its parts. You can make this with Bramley apples if you don't have quinces, or even a mixture of the two.

N

Serves 6

Ingredients

6 quinces, skinned, cored and quartered, or 6 cooking apples, cored and chopped

Juice of ½ lemon (if using quinces)

2 tablespoons demerara sugar (if using quinces)

280ml maple syrup

200g short-grain pudding rice

900ml full fat milk

900ml double cream

100g golden caster sugar

Seeds of 1 vanilla pod

25g butter, diced

Freshly grated nutmeg

Method

If you are using apples instead of quinces, skip this step. Drop the prepared quinces into boiling water with the lemon juice and demerara sugar. Simmer for about 25 minutes, or until a skewer goes into the flesh easily. Drain and leave to cool until they are easy to handle, then chop into 1–2cm chunks.

Put the cooked quince or raw apple into a saucepan with 170ml maple syrup and bring to the boil, stirring until the syrup and juices bubble and evaporate, leaving just a sticky coating to the fruit.

Put the rice, milk, cream, sugar, 60ml maple syrup and vanilla seeds into a saucepan and bring to the boil. Reduce to a simmer and cook for about 20–25 minutes, stirring, until the rice is cooked and the mixture thickened.

Preheat the oven to 190°C, Gas Mark 5 and generously butter a 20 x 23cm ovenproof dish. Spread the quince or apple across the base of the dish and pour the rice pudding over it. Dot with the butter and drizzle on the rest of the maple syrup. Grate nutmeg over the top and bake the pudding for 30 minutes. Allow it to sit for 10 minutes before eating.

FOLK STORY OF THE MONTH

The Laird of Balmachie's Wife

We think of fairies as sweet, happy little creatures but in the past it was well understood that they were wicked. They were particularly known for swapping healthy human babies for their own sickly changelings. Luckily, fairy folk that are up to no good can be stopped by being thrown onto the fire. No effigies for them – on they go, shawl, bonnet and all. This is what happens in this tale from Dumfries and Galloway in Scotland.

Many years ago, the Laird of Balmachie was required to ride to Dundee on business. His wife was ill and so stayed at home in bed. As the laird was returning, dusk was falling, so he took a short cut in order to reach home before dark. As he rode along, he spotted a troop of fairies on the hillside, carrying a sedan chair. He sensed that they were up to no good, so he drew his sword and galloped up the hillside after them, shouting, 'In the name of God, release your captive!' The tiny troop and chair vanished and a woman fell into the damp heather. Rushing over, the laird was astonished to see that it was his own wife, dressed in her nightclothes, confused and chilly but otherwise unhurt.

They rode back to their castle and the lady went to bed in a warm bedroom. He then went to her bedchamber, where he had left her that morning. There he found a very sickly and pale version of his wife, sitting there complaining about how she had been neglected and cold all day. 'Here, wife, let me build up the fire for you,' said the laird, and he heaped logs onto the fire until it was roaring. 'Now, come a little closer to the fire and we will warm you up,' said the laird. The lady refused, and so the laird lifted her out of bed, carried her to the fire and threw her onto it. She landed in the flames and then immediately flew straight up into the air, bursting a hole in the roof.

Fairies were never seen again around the laird's house, but although the hole in the roof was well mended, once each year a great wind would blow up that would damage that one piece, and no other, requiring it to be mended all over again.

N

FOLK SONG OF THE MONTH

'Cob-coaling'
Traditional, arr. Richard Barnard

This Bonfire Night song is from the Lancashire and Yorkshire border and is thought to have once been part of a mummers' play. It refers to the tradition of cob-coaling in the run-up to Bonfire Night, when children went from door to door singing cob-coaling songs to ask for lumps of wood and coal, and money for fireworks. The practice of cob-coaling is thought to have died out in the 1980s. More recently, however, it was a street song, sometimes sung by children asking for 'a penny for the Guy' as they carted around an effigy of Guy Fawkes they'd made from old rags, which would eventually be thrown on the bonfire – another custom that has generally disappeared. The song contains a snippet of the nursery rhyme 'Remember, Remember the Fifth of November', which is still chanted by the Lewes Bonfire Societies.

We come a cob-coaling for Bonfire Time,
Your coal and your money we hope you enjoy.
Fal-a-dee, fal-a-die, fal-a-diddle-die-do-day

Now down in your cellar there's an old umbrella,
There's nowt in yon corner but an old pepper box.
Pepper box, pepper box, morning till night;
If you give us nowt, we'll take nowt and bid you good night!
Fol-a-dee, fol-a-die, fol-a-diddle-die-do-day

Remember, remember the fifth of November
For gunpowder, treason should never be forgot.
We'll knock at your knocker and ring at your bell
and see what you give us for singing so well.
Fol-a-dee, fol-a-die, fol-a-diddle-die-do-day

♩. = 56

We come a cob-coal-ing for Bon-fire___ Time, your coal and your mo-ney we

hope you en - joy. *Fol - a - dee, fol - a - die, fol - a - did-dle-die - do - day* Now

down in your cel - lar there's an old um - br - el - la, there's

nowt in yon cor - ner but an old pep-per box. Pep-per box, pep-per box,

morn-ing til night; If you give us nowt, we'll take nowt and bid you good night! *Fol - a -*

dee, fol - a - die, fol - a - did-dle-die - do - day Re - mem-ber, re-mem-ber the

fifth of No-vem-ber for gun-pow-der trea-son should ne-ver be for-got. We'll

knock at your knock-er and ring at your bell and see what you give us for

sing-ing so well. *Fol - a - dee, fol - a - die, fol - a - did-dle-die - do - day*

NATURE

Bird of the month – starling

This is the month to see starlings in all their glory. A murmuration (from a medieval Latin word meaning 'murmuring' or 'grumbling') of starlings is one of the wonders of the natural world, a mass of swooping and swirling birds that blackens the sky, and they start appearing this month. During the winter, starlings have daytime roosts in high perches where they can see all around for predators, but at night they gather in huge numbers to roost in areas with plentiful supplies of food. Before they settle for the night, they set off in their great swooping clouds, moving almost as one, like a shoal of fish, creating huge columns, swirls and twists in the sky. Scientists have discovered that each bird in the murmuration tracks the seven birds closest to it and copies their movements, and this is why we see a sort of ripple of movement through them.

Starlings on their own are far less majestic. Dark and speckled all over, they are a little smaller than blackbirds and are a bit scruffy-looking. They make a variety of sounds that, on the whole, are not particularly musical and are a little on the screechy side, but that also include buzzes and trills and mimicry of other birds and of the sounds around them. If you can't get out to a wetland or reserve to see the murmurations, you may well see starlings in smaller gangs on your lawn, which they will probe in search of earthworms.

In spring the male builds a basic nest and then puffs himself up and sings to attract a mate. When she comes near, he waves his wings, fans his tail and hunches his back. Hopefully entranced, she will then complete the nest. By some unknown mechanism and for some inexplicable reason, if there are several pairs of starlings nesting within an area, these community-minded birds will synchronise their laying, perhaps increasing the chances of success for the collective.

STARLING

N

December

1 Start of meteorological winter

18 FIFA 2022 World Cup Final, Lusail Iconic Stadium, Qatar – 15.00 (GMT)

18 Hanukkah – festival of lights (Jewish) – begins at sundown

21 Winter solstice – start of astronomical winter

21 Yule/Midwinter/Midwinter's Day (traditional, pagan, neopagan)

24 Christmas Eve (Christian)

25 Christmas Day (Christian)

26 Boxing Day/St Stephen's Day (Christian) – bank holiday England, Wales, Scotland, Northern Ireland, Ireland

27 Bank holiday in lieu of Christmas Day – England, Wales, Scotland, Northern Ireland

31 New Year's Eve

DRESSING UP IN DECEMBER

The 'Wren Boys' of Ireland

On St Stephen's Day, 26th December, in towns and villages along the west coast of Ireland, people will dress up in straw suits and hats that cover their faces to 'hunt the wren'. Although no birds are now harmed, wrens were once actually hunted as part of the custom. Tied to the end of a long pole, they were carried through the streets as the bearers knocked on doors and asked for money to bury the wren. The donors would receive a feather from the bird, for luck, as sailors and fishermen believed that those who possessed a wren's feather would never be shipwrecked. Traditionally, this money was used to throw a 'Wren's Ball', sometime in January.

The hunting of the wren is a curiously widespread custom, most common in Ireland but with variants on the Isle of Man and in Pembrokeshire, as well as in southern France and Galicia in northwest Spain. This is particularly odd as throughout Europe wrens have long been considered lucky and sacred – they are called king of the birds in several European languages – and to kill one was thought to bring bad luck. Nobody quite knows what it all means, but there are plenty of theories.

The wren has long been associated with winter because it sings on through the darkest months. This led to a belief that it could be slain and brought back to life, a symbol – much like the evergreen foliage with which we deck our halls – of the triumph of light over darkness, and life over death. The Celtic name for wren is *dreoilín*, which some have conjectured could come from *draoi ean*, or 'druid's bird', so perhaps the tradition arose from some sort of ritualised sacrifice. Wrens also represent the old year, so this may be the logic behind killing one as the year ends. On yet another hand, it may have arisen because it was the wren that betrayed St Stephen to his enemies by singing in the bush in which he was hiding (*dreoilín* also means 'trickster').

Now, happily, a stuffed or fake wren, adorned with ribbons is tied to a holly bush on a stick. It is carried from door to door while the 'wren boys' sing (see page 262) and dance and collect money. A tradition steeped in mystery, to end the year.

THE SKY

Mars is at opposition – essentially a 'full Mars' – and in the same part of the sky as Jupiter. It will also get so close to the full moon that it will be 'occulted' by it, disappearing for an hour. Later, we have the impressive Geminids meteor shower, with up to 120 meteors per hour at its peak.

At night

1st: Conjunction of Jupiter and the moon. They will appear at around 16.30 and will set around midnight in the west.

7th–8th: Conjunction of Mars and the full moon and occultation of Mars. Appearing together at around 16.20 on the 7th low in the northeast, they will reach a maximum altitude at midnight. At around 05.00 on the 8th, Mars will disappear behind the moon and will reappear an hour later.

8th: Mars at opposition. It will be at its highest and brightest, and closest to earth.

13th–14th: Geminids meteor shower. The peak will be at around 02.00 on the morning of the 14th but you should see trails for several hours before and after. The moon will obscure the fainter meteors.

29th: Conjunction of Jupiter and the moon. They will appear in the dusk at around 16.30 at an altitude of 35 degrees in the south. Visible until setting at 23.00 in the west.

By day

21st: The winter solstice falls at 21.48, the moment that the sun is directly overhead at the Tropic of Capricorn, the southernmost latitude at which it can be directly overhead.

21st: At solar noon the sun will reach an altitude of 15 degrees in the London sky and 11 degrees in the Glasgow sky.

1st–31st: Day length decreases this month by 27m up to the solstice on the 21st, and then increases by 6m by the end of the month, at Clitheroe, Lancashire.

Sunrise and set
Clitheroe, Lancashire

	01	02	03	04	05	06	07	08	09	10	11	12	13	14	15	16	17	18	19	20	21	22	23	24
1st																								
2nd																								
3rd																								
4th																								
5th																								
6th																								
7th																								
8th																								
9th																								
10th																								
11th																								
12th																								
13th																								
14th																								
15th																								
16th																								
17th																								
18th																								
19th																								
20th																								
21st							Winter solstice																	
22nd																								
23rd																								
24th																								
25th																								
26th																								
27th																								
28th																								
29th																								
30th																								
31st																								

Deep-sky objects

The Double Cluster

The Double Cluster is best viewed in winter, when the Perseus constellation is high in the sky. It is about 7,500 light years away from us, on the Perseus Arm of the Milky Way (see page 123), while we are on the Orion Arm. The two clusters are just a few hundred light years apart from each other.

To find the Double Cluster, first find Perseus and look nearby for Cassiopeia, with its distinctive 'W' shape, then scan between them to spot two soft blurs. Once you have found them, look through binoculars and you may pick out many of the young, hot, blue-white super giants, each thousands of times brighter than our sun. If the Double Cluster was as close to us as the Pleiades (444 light years) it would cover a quarter of our night sky and provide us with some of our brightest stars. As it is, together the clusters occupy about twice the space of a full moon in our night sky.

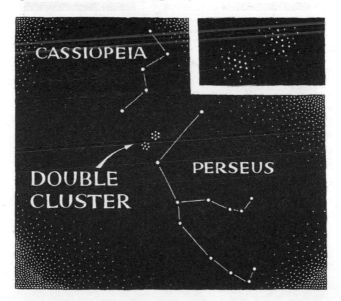

THE SEA

Average sea temperature

Shetland:	9.8°C
Greenock:	10.0°C
Cleethorpes:	8.3°C
Rhyl:	9.7°C
Rosslare:	11.3°C
Bideford:	11.3°C
Deal:	10.7°C

Spring and neap tides

Spring tides are the most extreme tides of the month, with the highest rises and the lowest falls, and they follow a couple of days after the full moon and new moon. There will be a super new moon (when the new moon coincides with the moment in the month when the moon is closest to the earth) on the 23rd so the spring tides that follow it may be more extreme than usual. Neap tides are the least extreme tides of the month, with the smallest movement, and they fall in between the spring tides.

Spring tides: 9th–11th and 24th–26th

Neap tides: 1st–2nd and 17th–18th

Spring tides are shaded in black in the chart opposite.

December tide timetable for Dover

For guidance on how to convert this for your local area, see page 8.

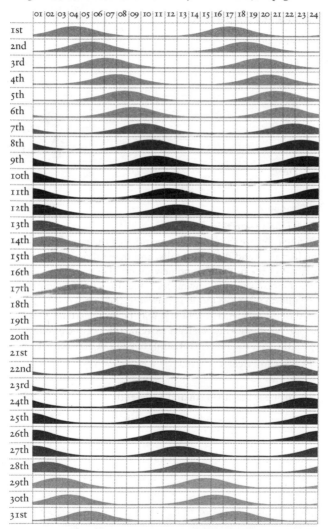

THE MOON

Moon phases

Full moon – 8th December, 04.08

3rd quarter – 16th December, 08.56

New moon – 23rd December, 10.16

1st quarter – 30th December, 01.20

Full moon
Names for December's full moon: Moon Before Yule, Oak Moon, Full Cold Moon.

New moon
This month's new moon is in Capricorn. Astrologers believe that the new moon is a good time to make plans and focus on your dreams and hopes for the period ahead, and that each new moon has a particular energy, depending on which zodiacal sign it is in. The Capricorn new moon, which falls on the 23rd, is said to rule ambitions and goals, making this a good time to think about career plans and changes and how you can start to work towards them.

Moon phases for December

1st	2nd	3rd	4th	5th

6th	7th	8th FULL	9th	10th

11th	12th	13th	14th	15th

16th	17th	18th	19th	20th

21st	22nd	23rd NEW	24th	25th

26th	27th	28th	29th	30th

31st				

THE GARDEN

Gardening by the moon

We have reached the darkest point in the year. The winter solstice – the shortest day and longest night – falls on the 21st, and the garden feels closed down, deep in slumber. One old piece of weather lore says, 'The nearer the new moon to Christmas Day, the harder the winter'. With this month's new moon falling on the 23rd, we might be in for frost and snow in the months ahead. But even in the few weeks following the solstice, light will noticeably increase, and the garden will feel it. There will soon be little signs of life, hints of the busy spring season to come, so enjoy this winter rest and the opportunity it brings to get the garden into shape.

Whether you are gardening in time with the moon or not, use the following as a guide to jobs to do in December.

Note: Sometimes these dates differ from those in the moon phase chart on page 253, to take into account sensible gardening hours. Where no specific time for the change between phases is mentioned, this is because it happens early in the morning or late at night. For exact changeover times for any late-night or pre-dawn gardening, refer to the moon phase chart.

1st quarter to full moon: 30th November (from 14.36)–7th, and 30th–6th Jan 2023
Sow crops that develop above ground, don't sow root crops. Plant out seedlings and young plants. Take cuttings and make grafts. Avoid other pruning. Fertilise.
- Take grafts of favourite apple varieties to make new young plants.

Full moon to 3rd quarter: 8th–15th
A 'drawing down' energy. Sow and plant crops that develop below ground: root crops, bulbs and perennials.
- Plant garlic cloves.
- Plant rhubarb crowns. Lift, split and replant large clumps.

- Plant new fruit bushes and trees. Apples, pears, cherries, plums, quinces, medlars, apricots, peaches, nectarines and all soft-fruit bushes can be planted now.
- Plant new perennials in your flower borders, and lift, divide and replant any that are a few years old.

3rd quarter to new moon: 16th–23rd (till 10.16)

A dormant period, with low sap and poor growth. Do not sow or plant. Prune, weed and harvest crops for storage. Fertilise and mulch. Garden maintenance.

- Prune apple, pear, medlar and quince trees.
- Prune grapevines before the winter solstice.
- Check your soil for its pH level. If it is low, add lime or calcified seaweed.
- Mulch beds with organic manure.
- Weed thoroughly. This is a good time to get ahead with any perennial weed problems.
- Prune roses.
- Put terracotta pots on 'pot feet' to lift them from the ground and improve drainage, ahead of the very cold months ahead.
- Order seed for next year.

New moon to 1st quarter: 23rd (from 10.16)–29th

Rising vitality and upward growth. Plant and sow anything that develops above ground towards the end of phase. Prepare for growth.

- Sow microgreens on a windowsill: basil, dill, celery, onion, chervil, beetroot, coriander, red mustard and pea. Harvest when 5cm tall.

NATURE

Bird of the month – wren

In many years, wrens are among the most common birds in our landscape, but you wouldn't know it. They owe their success to their ability to thrive in a great variety of habitats, from gardens to remote cliff edges to farmland and heathlands. And they owe their mystery to their diminutive size and ability to quickly dart in among foliage and hide themselves, a trait that has earned them a reputation as tricksters in mythology around the world.

At just 9–10cm long and weighing about the same as a £1 coin, they are tiny but not quite the tiniest: the firecrest and goldcrest are smaller. Wrens are exceptionally cute, though, being almost round with short wings and a perky, cocked-up tail.

For such little birds, wrens have a startlingly loud song – lyrical and trembling, with each five-second phrase usually ending in a trill. They can make so much noise from such a small body because of an organ called a syrinx, which has a resonating chamber and membranes that amplify the sound and allow them to sing two notes at one time. They can sing right through winter, which is perhaps one of the reasons why they have become associated with winter in folklore. In Dutch they are called *winterkoning* – 'winter king'. In fact, a harsh winter can be very hard on them, and this is when their numbers can plummet. One survival mechanism they have is of roosting together to keep warm. If a wren has found a particularly cosy nook on a cold day, it will suspend any territorial hostilities with other wrens in the area and will make brief flights, putting out a call to announce vacancies. Up to 60 wrens have been seen cramming into a standard-sized nest box, their heads facing inwards, using their body heat to keep each other warm, like tiny feathered penguins.

When spring comes, the male wren will build up to 12 domed nests low down in a tree crevice or in a thick wall of ivy, and then invite his chosen female to select one.

WREN

THE KITCHEN

The run-up to and aftermath of Christmas can be charted in food and drink: the first chocolate Advent calendar window; a mince pie while you make your lists; a sparkling evening or two of canapés and champagne; carol singing with mulled wine; the great feast itself; and the glorious lazing around with leftovers.

Hanukkah also falls this month, its celebration of the miracle of the oil translated in the kitchen into deep-fried *sufganiyot* (jam-filled doughnuts), *knish* (small savoury pastries) and *latkes* (potato pancakes). We must also find a moment to mark the winter solstice, and the turning of the year back towards the light, perhaps with a mug of mulled cider and a *waes hael* (the Saxon greeting that became 'wassail').

In season

In the hedgerows, woods and fields
Wild fruits and nuts: Crab apples, sweet chestnuts
Roots: Alexanders, dandelion, horseradish, Jerusalem artichokes, lovage, rampion, wild garlic
Wild greens: Chickweed, hairy bittercress, dandelion leaves, sow thistle, wintercress/yellow rocket
Game: Hare, pheasant, rabbit, venison

From the seashore and rivers
Fish and shellfish: Mussels, oysters, turbot, black bream, herring

From the kitchen garden
Fruits: Quinces
Vegetables: Beetroot, Brussels sprouts, cabbages, carrots, cauliflowers, celeriac, celery, chard, chicory, garlic, kale, leeks, lettuces, onions, Oriental leaves, spring onions, parsnips, potatoes, pumpkins, winter squashes, spinach, swedes, turnips
Herbs: Chervil, parsley, coriander, sage, rosemary, bay

From the farms
Stilton, goose, turkey

RECIPES

Biscuit of the month

Walnut, cranberry and ginger Florentines

These make beautiful edible Christmas gifts, or they can be kept in the biscuit tin for those odd callers who don't like mince pies.

Makes 8
Ingredients
50g butter
50g plain flour
50g golden syrup
50g golden caster sugar
50g cranberries
75g walnuts, toasted and roughly chopped
50g crystallised ginger, roughly chopped
Zest of 1 orange
100g plain dark or white chocolate (optional)

Method
Preheat the oven to 180°C, Gas Mark 4. Line 2 baking sheets with nonstick baking paper. Put the butter, flour, golden syrup and sugar in a saucepan over a medium heat, stirring until the butter has melted and the mixture is smooth. Add the cranberries, walnuts, ginger and zest. Stir well, then put 4 tablespoons of the mixture onto each baking sheet with plenty of space between them to spread out. Bake for 12–14 minutes and leave to cool for a few minutes on the baking sheets before transferring them to a cooling rack. Once the biscuits are cool, melt the dark or white chocolate in a bowl over hot water, and drizzle over the biscuits or dip the biscuits in the melted chocolate – or leave them plain if you prefer.

Mini kimchi sausage rolls

Keep party guests happy with these sausage rolls spiked with hot and sour kimchi. Vary the ratio of kimchi to sausagemeat according to how hot your kimchi is and how spicy you want the rolls to be, always ending up with 650g of filling. You can also make this into six larger sausage rolls for a hearty lunch.

Makes 20 mini or 6 medium
Ingredients
300g kimchi (weight when drained and patted dry), chopped
350g sausagemeat
320g packet pre-rolled puff pastry
1 egg, beaten
Black onion seeds, for sprinkling
Salt and pepper

Method
Preheat the oven to 200°C, Gas Mark 6. Line a baking sheet with nonstick baking paper. Put the kimchi in a bowl with the sausagemeat. Season well with salt and pepper, and mix with your hands for a couple of minutes, giving the meat a good pummel and squeezing to tenderise it.

Lay out one pastry sheet on a lightly floured surface and cut it in half lengthways. Roll one piece lightly widthways to make it wider. Form half of the meat mixture into a roll and place it down the centre of the pastry. Brush egg along one edge of the pastry. Roll it up from the other edge, and place it so the seam is underneath. Cut the roll into 3cm pieces and arrange on the baking sheet. Repeat for the other piece of pastry and the rest of the meat mixture. Paint the tops and sides with the beaten egg, then sprinkle a pinch of black onion seeds onto each.

Bake for about 25–30 minutes or until golden brown on the bottom as well as top – they are better when really crunchy, so overcook rather than undercook. Serve as soon as they are cool enough to handle.

FOLK STORY OF THE MONTH

How the Wren Became King of the Birds

Despite its diminutive size, the wren is known as the king of
the birds, and is also considered tricky and cunning, perhaps
partly because of its ability to quickly flit and disappear into a
hedgerow. Here is how it got its name, and its reputation.

Once upon a time, all of the birds gathered together for a
race to decide who among them was king of the birds. It was
decided that whichever bird could fly the highest would be
crowned. They all took off in a great beating of wings, flying
straight upwards towards the sun. Up and up they flew, but
soon the smaller birds were exhausted, as their little wings
had beaten so many times, and they fell away from the pack
and flew back down to earth. Gradually the ducks, the gulls,
the crows and even the owls drifted back down to the ground,
defeated. And so it went on until there was one single huge
eagle still beating its wings skyward. Finally, worn out and
triumphant, he started to glide downwards, at which the little
wren popped out from where he had been clinging onto the
underside of one of the eagle's wings. Entirely rested from
hitching a ride, he flew up above the exhausted eagle, who now
had no energy to fly any higher, and sang, 'I am the king! I am
the king!'
   All of the birds were astonished when they heard the
news, as they hadn't expected so tiny a bird to win. The
eagle was furious. 'I used all of my strength to win,' he said.
'I should be king!' But the wren said, 'If the eagle can win
through his strength, why can I not win through my cunning
and cleverness?' And so the matter was settled.

FOLK SONG OF THE MONTH

'The Wren Song'
Traditional, arr. Richard Barnard

This is the song sung by the 'wren boys' (see page 246) as they parade the streets on St Stephen's Day, 26th December. Wren is pronounced 'wran'.

Fast ♩. = 132

The wren, the wren, the king of all birds St Ste-phen's Day was caught in the furze. Although he was lit-tle his ho-nour was great, jump up, my lads and give us a treat. As
I was go-ing to Kil-le-naule I met a wren u-pon a wall, up with my wat-tle and
knocked him down and brought him in to Car-rick Town. "Dreoi-lín, dreoi-lín,
where's your nest?" "Tis in the bush that I love best; in the tree, the
hol-ly tree, where all the boys do fol-low me." Up with the ket-tle and
down with the pan and give us a pen-ny to bu-ry the wren.

The wren, the wren, the king of all birds
St Stephen's Day was caught in the furze,
Although he was little his honour was great,
Jump up, my lads and give us a treat.

As I was going to Killenaule,
I met a wren upon a wall,
Up with my wattle and knocked him down
And brought him in to Carrick Town.

'Dreoilín, dreoilín, where's your nest?'
''Tis in the bush that I love best;
In the tree, the holly tree,
Where all the boys do follow me.'
Up with the kettle and down with the pan
And give us a penny to bury the wren.

I followed the wren three miles or more,
Three miles or more, three miles or more
I followed the wren three miles or more
At six-o-clock in the morning.

I have a box here under my arm,
Here under my arm, here under my arm.
I have a box here under my arm,
A penny or tuppence would do it no harm.

Mrs Quinn's a very good woman
A very good woman, a very good woman
Mrs Quinn's a very good woman
She'll give us a penny to bury the wren.
Up with the kettle and down with the pan
And give us a penny to bury the wren.

D

FURTHER READING

Besson, Gérard A, *Folklore and Legends of Trinidad and Tobago*, Port of Spain: Paria Publishing, 2007

Bourne, Henry, *Arcadia Britannica: A Modern British Folklore Portrait*, London: Thames & Hudson, 2015

Hannant, Sara, *Mummers, Maypoles and Milkmaids: A Journey Through the English Ritual Year*, London: Merrell Publishers, 2011

Hutton, Ronald, *The Stations of the Sun: A History of the Ritual Year in Britain*, Oxford: Oxford University Press, 1996

Kerven, Rosalind, *English Fairy Tales and Legends*, London: Batsford, 2019

Magnusson, Magnus, *The Complete Book of British Birds*, Basingstoke: Automobile Association, 1992

Marshall, Sybil, *The Book of English Folk Tales*, London: Duckworth, 2016

Roberts, Jem, *Tales of Britain*, unbound digital, 2019

Roud, Steve, *The English Year: A Month-by-Month Guide to the Nation's Customs and Festivals, from May Day to Mischief Night*, London: Penguin Books, 2008

RESOURCES

Abbots Bromley Horn Dance: abbotsbromley.com/information/horn_dance/

Bankside Twelfth Night celebrations: www.thelionspart.co.uk

Easy Tide: www.ukho.gov.uk/easytide

English Folk Dance and Song Society: www.efdss.org

Lewes Bonfire Societies: lewesbonfirecouncil.org.uk

The London Pearly Kings and Queens Society: www.pearlysociety.co.uk

Messier objects: www.messier-objects.com

Music hall and coster songs directory: folksongandmusichall.com

Notting Hill Carnival: nhcarnival.org

The Pearly Kings and Queens of St Pancras: thepearlies.org.uk

Wrea Green Rose Queens: wreagreen.com

ACKNOWLEDGEMENTS

Thank you to everyone who has helped me to create this almanac.

Many thanks to Allyson Williams MBE and Symone Williams of Notting Hill Carnival and Genesis Mas Band for sharing your knowledge on the folklore and traditions of Carnival.

Thanks to John Walters, the Pearly King of Finsbury, for information on the Pearly Kings and Queens Harvest Festivals, and to John Baxter of www.folksongandmusichall.com for advice and guidance on music hall and on coster songs in particular.

Thanks as ever to Richard Barnard, who puts the music together so carefully and creatively, and to my dad, Jack Leendertz, for taking care of the sky at night sections so diligently.

I was delighted that Harry Brockway agreed to illustrate the almanac this year and it has been a joy seeing his wonderful illustrations emerge. Thank you for all your beautiful work, Harry.

Extra special thanks to the almanac's designer Matt Cox of Newman+Eastwood this year, who has had the additional task of revamping the tables, taking my series of sketches and turning them into something clean and stylish. Thank you so much for all of the work you put in on this. I think they are wonderful.

Huge thanks to everyone at Octopus who puts the almanac together and supports it once it is out in the world: Stephanie Jackson, Jonathan Christie, Ella Parsons, Matt Grindon, Karen Baker, Alison Wormleighton and Jane Birch. Thanks to my agent, Adrian Sington at Kruger Cowne.

Last but not least, thank you to my gorgeous family, Michael, Rowan and Meg, with a special mention this year to Meg, whose stray comment led to me entirely rethinking all of the tables. Thanks sweetie!

REFERENCES

Astronomical and calendarial information reproduced with permission from HM Nautical Almanac Office (HMNAO), UK Hydrographic Office (UKHO) and the Controller of Her Majesty's Stationery Office.

Sunrises and sunsets and further calculations reproduced with permission from www.timeanddate.com.

Tidal predictions reproduced with permission from HMNAO, UKHO and the Controller of Her Majesty's Stationery Office.

Astronomical events are based on ephemerides obtained using the NASA JPL Horizons system.

Sea temperatures are reproduced with permission from www.seatemperatures.org.

INDEX